Contents

ug Your Business!

larketing on MySpace, YouTube, blogs and podcasts

1d other Web 2.0 social networks

Steve Weber

Plug Your Business!

Marketing on MySpace, YouTube, blogs and podcasts and other Web 2.0 social networks

Weber Books
Falls Church, Va.
www.WeberBooks.com

By Steve Weber
All Rights Reserved © 2007 by Stephen W. Weber

Published by Stephen W. Weber
Printed in the United States of America
Weber Books   www.WeberBooks.com

Author: Steve Weber
Editor: Julie Bird

13-digit ISBN: 978-0-9772406-2-3
10-digit ISBN: 0-9772406-2-2

Front cover photo: Copyright 2007 JupiterImages Corp.

Warning and Disclaimer

The information in this book is offered with the understanding that it does not contain legal, financial, or other professional advice. Individuals requiring such services should consult a competent professional.

The author and publisher make no representations about the suitability of the information contained in this book for any purpose. This material is provided "as is" without warranty of any kind.

Although every effort has been made to ensure the accuracy of the contents of this book, errors and omissions can occur. The publisher assumes no responsibility for any damages arising from the use of this book, or alleged to have resulted in connection with this book.

This book is not completely comprehensive. Some readers may wish to consult additional books for advice. Additional sources of information are identified in the appendices of this book.

This book is not endorsed by any of the companies mentioned in the text.

Introduction

No matter what kind of business you have, its success depends on two things: It must serve a need, and you must find customers.

Most new businesses fail simply because the right people never heard about them. And this is the paradox for entrepreneurs: People aren't paying attention to traditional marketing and advertising anymore. But *free* advertising is alive and well. Whatever you want to call it—buzz, word of mouth, peer-to-peer or viral marketing—you can't just manufacture it. You must earn it—by engaging your target market.

Fortunately, there is a very straightforward, ethical way of gaining this free exposure: by participating on social networks. These social media sites, such as MySpace and other Web 2.0 networks, allow members to create profiles of themselves (or their business) with the objective of meeting like-minded friends and partners who share the same passions and goals.

The individuals participating on these networks might be searching for anything—a mentor, a ride to work, a date for Saturday night, recommendations for a movie, a new job, or perhaps they want to meet someone who's an expert in their hobby. For business owners who learn to use them, social networks can provide valuable free exposure to a worldwide pool of new customers and fans.

These social networks have turned traditional marketing on its head. No longer must a business owner scrape together a huge pile of cash for a marketing campaign, then pray that it works. Hundreds of thousands of businesses large and small are leveraging social networks to lure new customers, often at virtually no cost.

And unlike most traditional advertising, social networking can pay dividends for years to come because it forges a strong link between you and consumers, enabling your biggest fans to become evangelists for your business.

Internet social networks allow entrepreneurs to build their businesses one customer at a time. It's the same as having a "street team" pounding the pavement for you. Just as your street team might pass out fliers about a show or new product, your MySpace friends can forward the same type of information using electronic messages to a much larger audience. When you're successful, your loyal customers begin spreading the word for you, generating true word of mouth.

Entrepreneurs can no longer depend on interruption-based ads, such as commercials and junk mail, which force consumers to stop what they're doing and pay attention. But with social networking, you can influence these consumers precisely at the point where they're engaged.

In the old days, with postal direct mail or telephone cold-calling, your chance of getting a response from someone who didn't know you was about 2 percent—and that's if you had a big marketing budget and were doing *everything* right. But today, the social-networking skills described in this book can result in response rates of 80 percent or more.

With these powerful new tools, it's important to learn the ropes because marketing with social media is a double-edged sword. A single member of the community you're targeting has a voice just as loud as yours. Yes, if the community likes you, they'll help spread the word about you better than a million-dollar ad campaign. On the other hand, one disgruntled customer might be even more motivated—and effective—in voicing a contrary opinion.

What others are doing

This book contains many examples of the current uses of social networking. MySpace currently leads the pack for now, but newer sites and opportunities are coming online every day. While each site is different, the basic features and dynamics are similar on each, and the same marketing principles apply across the board: You can help your business by helping potential customers connect, belong, discover, and build knowledge.

Social networking sites of today boast millions of users segmented by interest, geography and age. They offer marketers an unprecedented opportunity for marketing because it enables your target market to *find you*, instead of you finding them. No longer must marketers blast advertisements to people who aren't paying attention.

Marketing on social-networking sites is refreshingly simple and pays obvious dividends. You choose a network that caters to your intended audience. You create a profile and lure customers by providing content interesting to them. With the proper effort, any marketing objective can be achieved—to introduce or reinforce your brand image, inspire customer loyalty, or simply drive visitors to your Web site, Internet store, or affiliated retailer.

The best way to determine how your business can benefit from social networking is to view some examples of what others are doing:

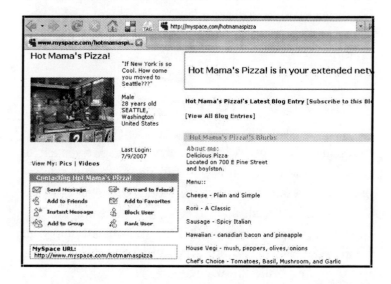

Hot Mama's Pizza—www.myspace.com/hotmamas pizza.

This family restaurant in Seattle uses a free MySpace profile to displays its menu, list of pizza toppings, street address, and phone number for free delivery. "If New York is so cool, how come you moved to Seattle?" the profile asks visitors.

It's a good idea to encourage your customers to add their personal "success stories" about your products or services as they visit your Web pages. One comment from a customer says, "You make the best pizza in town."

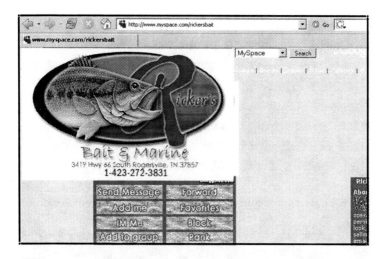

Ricker's Bait—www.myspace.com/rickersbait. The MySpace profile for this bait and tackle shop in rural Tennessee features a slide show of local fishermen with their prize catches. The page includes the hours and phone number of the shop, details on fishing seasons and tournaments, and links to forums and a newsletter.

Dasani FruitSigns–www.myspace.com/fruitsigns.
Coca-Cola's Dasani unit promotes its Fruit Signs brand on
this MySpace profile. Users enter their birth year and
receive a "Fruit Sign" of lemon, raspberry, grape or
strawberry. A quiz determines which other signs the user
is compatible with, and users receive a widget to display
the results on their profile. Users also receive a customized MySpace layout that advertises Dasani.

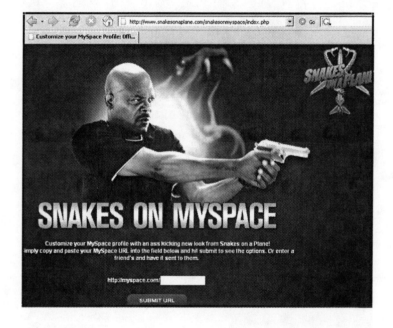

Snakes on a Plane – www.snakesoneaplane.com/
snakesonmyspace. New Line Cinema created this stand-
alone Web site, often called a "microsite" to advertise
"Snakes on a Plane." Visitors submitted the URL of their
MySpace profile to receive their own movie-themed
MySpace layout, sometimes called a "custom skin." New
Line also posted "viral" video clips about the film on
YouTube. A microsite can serve as a hub for a larger cross-

media campaign involving television, billboards and print ads directing viewers to the Web site. By contrast, a campaign limited to a social-networking profile is more limiting, but enables you to attract a more targeted audience. Although the online campaign succeeded in raising awareness of the movie, "Snakes" bombed at the box office, providing that awareness doesn't always prompt consumption, particularly in the entertainment industry.

Social games and contests are particularly effective because they can prompt consumers to not only remember a product or company, but recommend it to friends. Cadbury Schweppes used an innovative game to promote its Dr. Pepper soft drink. The company hid game coins worth up to $1 million in public areas in 23 cities. Clues to the location of the coins were available on the "Hunt for More" Web site to players who got codes out of Dr. Pepper containers.

Les Cross & Associates— www.myspace.com/attorney_cross.

Texas-based entertainment lawyer Leslie Warren Cross launched this MySpace.com page in 2006, wondering whether it would help him drum up business. He used the page to provide up-and-coming musicians basic information about the legalities of music contracts. Indeed, Cross says that as he acquired "friends" on his MySpace page, he noticed that the site was bringing in new clients for his firm, Les Cross & Associates, and a way to stay in contact with his vagabond musician clients.

On MySpace, Cross calls himself Music Attorney Cross (The Street Fighter) the same sort of "tough guy" image as the rap-music clients he's targeting. He believes it's an effective way to reach younger prospective clients who seldom search through traditional media like telephone directories and newspapers seeking a lawyer.

The Hub—www.schoolyourway.walmart.com .
One of the most spectacular social-networking flops was

launched in 2006 by retailing giant Wal-Mart and canceled just 10 weeks later. The site was aimed at teens, featuring videos of young actors portraying "real" kids who enjoyed buying clothes at Wal-Mart. The site had practically no user-generated content and drew few "Hubsters." Experts believe the site failed because its content was so obviously phony.

Dell Computer—www.myspace.com/makeuswork. Dell Computer's MySpace profile provides free copies of its most popular "skins" for use as PC desktop wallpaper. Customer-service personnel monitor a forum to answer technical questions. A link forwards visitors to Dell's site for ordering custom-made computers.

Honda—www.myspace.com/hondaelement. To create buzz about its Element utility vehicle, Honda conducted an "Embrace MySpace" contest, asking members to create a background image to be featured on Honda's profile page.

Widget marketing

Most of the social-networking profiles mentioned here use some type of "widget"—a small icon that represents a business, and links to a Web page, video or some other place online.

Widget marketing reflects the physical world, such as someone who sports a bumper sticker for his favorite radio station. But with widget marketing, the reach is wider, the cost lower. Widget marketing is effective because it's often considered to be advice from a friend, not an advertisement.

Widgets are an important tool for viral marketing on social networks and blogs. Book publisher HarperCollins built this widget for the novel Twins. Fans of the author could click on the widget to view sample pages from the book, or download a snippet of HTML code to add the widget to their own blog or MySpace profile.

A Web widget is a mini tool—a chunk of code your friends can plug into their MySpace page or other profile. Widgets are usually a snippet of HTML code but can also use Adobe Flash or JavaScript programming languages. Some examples:

- An HTML image for MySpace users to plug into their profile.

- Code that embeds a YouTube video into a blog.

- HTML that embeds a calendar item on a Web site.

How to use this book

The beginning sections of this book explain the basics of online marketing using social networking, techniques that provide the most bang for your effort. As we proceed, some of the methods will be more complicated, requiring more skill and resources. Perhaps not everything discussed here will be practical for your book.

Your job is to select which promotional techniques might work best with your audience, and then use them aggressively and tirelessly. The more techniques you try, the better your chances of success. A single strategy won't work, but a combined effort will produce results, and the effect will be cumulative.

Many examples of Web sites are mentioned in this book. Take time to view these sites, instead of skimming ahead. Consider what you like and don't like about what other businesses have done, and apply the best ideas to your own efforts.

This book is not a get-rich-quick plan. It's a guide to promoting your existing business on social networking and Web 2.0 sites. It might require a year or more of steady work to see appreciable results. If that seems like a gamble and lots of work, it is. But the potential payoff is worth it. There is no such thing as overnight success.

Read through this entire book once. Then read it again, selecting and prioritizing what you'll tackle first. Mark on a calendar when you'll start each phase of your plan. Then get to it. Evaluate your progress after three months. Determine what's been successful, and redouble your efforts there. Then try something new.

MySpace buzz

When 24-year-old Steven Oliverez finished writing his debut fantasy novel, he faced the same predicament as most new authors. He wanted to sell the manuscript, but couldn't get a single publisher to *read it*, let alone buy it. He spent two years writing query letters, and all he got was a stack of form-letter rejections.

So Oliverez decided to self-publish and promote the book himself. Fortunately, he wasn't starting from scratch. He'd been active on the wildly popular social site MySpace, networking with other fantasy readers and authors. On his MySpace blog, he'd given away seven of his short stories to anyone willing to read them. His stories prompted hundreds of enthusiastic comments and attracted thousands of MySpace "friends."

So when Oliverez published *Elder Staves* in 2005, he asked for a little help from his MySpace friends. He asked them to buy the book on Amazon, and they did—pushing it to No. 25 on the fantasy bestseller list. Then Oliverez started getting messages from book clubs around the country, asking if he'd make phone-in appearances. After that came some write-ups in publishing trade magazines. Few tools can attract and bind an audience than a network like MySpace, Oliverez says:

> **"** Buzz creates more buzz. Since there's no marketing or publishing company behind the book, it really helps to be online, able to connect with readers directly. Being on MySpace makes you seem more approachable, and that makes it a great tool for authors.

Next Oliverez printed 30,000 personalized bookmarks, and asked his MySpace friends to pass them out at bookstores and coffee shops. Immediately he got a few dozen volunteers. Then Oliverez found more MySpace friends by joining several of its "groups" for authors and fiction-writing.

You can visit Oliverez on MySpace and read the first two chapters of his book at:

www.MySpace.com/Oliverez

Not just for kids anymore

What Oliverez did wasn't new. He took a page from the thousands of unsigned rock bands that have tapped MySpace to build their audiences. It's a simple yet wonderfully effective strategy: The bands put samples of their music on their MySpace profile, and friends forward the songs to an ever-enlarging circle of friends. Bands that "go viral" on MySpace sell lots more concert tickets and CDs, and some have snagged major recording contracts. Even the journeymen are raking it in by hawking their disks, T-shirts and other goodies right on MySpace.

MySpace Dominates Social Networking Usage, With Facebook A Distant Second

Percentage who use site at least weekly:

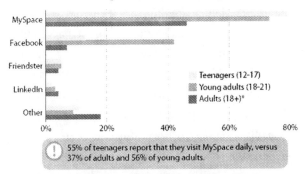

Teenagers (12-17)
Young adults (18-21)
Adults (18+)*

55% of teenagers report that they visit MySpace daily, versus 37% of adults and 56% of young adults.

Base: US online social networking site users
Source: Forrester's NACTAS Q4 2006 Youth Media & Marketing And Finance Online Survey
*Source: Forrester's NACTAS Q3 2006 Media & Marketing Online Survey

Social Networking Site Users Represent An Attractive And Viral Audience

Adult social networking site user demographics and psychographics

	Adult social networking site users	Site usage daily or more	Interested in marketer profiles
Mean age	37	32	33
Male	52.9%	52.8%	53.3%
Average household income (US$)	$63,390	$61,688	$63,595
College degree or higher	33%	28%	27%
Gen X (27-40)	43%	45%	49%
Read blogs weekly or more	34%	50%	50%
Publish own blog weekly or more	21%	39%	35%
Average number of social network sites used weekly or more	0.79	1.38	1.26
"I am a natural leader — people always listen to my opinion"*	33%	32%	49%
"I often tell my friends about products that interest me"*	50%	47%	61%
"I like to show off my taste and style"*	14%	18%	27%

Base: US adult online social network users
*Percentage of respondents who agree with this statement
Source: Forrester's NACTAS Q3 2006 Media & Marketing Online Survey

Illustrations reprinted with permission from "Marketing on Social Network Sites" by Charlene Li, Forrester Research, Inc., July 2007.

Authors—and many others who want to promote themselves or their business—are quickly realizing they can do the same thing the bands are doing: use MySpace to go directly to their potential customers without a big fat marketing campaign. New profiles on MySpace are created daily for artists, restaurants, movies, TV shows, bars, towns, and nearly any other thing imaginable. Used wisely, MySpace can provide genuine word of mouth for products and businesses at little or no cost.

Barely two years after its launch, MySpace became the most popular U.S. Web site based on number of visits during 2006. With nearly 100 million members, every target market is represented, already sliced and diced by interests and geography. Each MySpace member has his or her own circle of like-minded friends. After you become someone's MySpace friend, you have access to his or her friends. And each of your new friends has more friends.

While there are hundreds of social-networking sites— Facebook, Friendster, Orkut and Tribe.net to name just a few—MySpace has captured more than 80 percent of the traffic. To get started visit **www.MySpace.com** and click the "Sign Up" box on the right.

If you wish, you can make your MySpace account private until you're ready to use it. Go to **Account Settings** and then **Privacy Settings**.

MySpace? You might be thinking, "Isn't that for high-school kids?" Sure, that's the stereotype; MySpace is popular with kids. But with nearly 100 million members and the No. 1 traffic rank on the entire Internet, clearly there's more to it than loitering schoolkids.

All sorts of people are having success on MySpace. Horror novelist Michael Laimo says he got more than a dozen big media interviews after reporters noticed his MySpace page. He inked his first movie deal through

MySpace after an independent director sent him a MySpace message asking about film rights. Hundreds of fans have told him they bought his books after seeing his MySpace profile:

www.MySpace.com/MichaelLaimo

MySpace is the Internet's answer to a promotional tactic used by new entrepreneurs for decades—selling products from the trunk of your car. Both tactics are tedious, time-consuming, and usually don't produce results for a while. But if you keep plugging away and you're sincere, people notice. Your snowball starts barreling downhill purely from its own momentum.

Most MySpace members don't use the site as a promotion tool; they're just there to connect with friends. But MySpace can be a foolproof self-promotional tool if you're intent on using it that way. Any business owner, even one without computer skills, can easily post content that will draw interest from the target market.

In addition to its potential for promoting your business, MySpace is a wickedly good research tool. For example, in about 10 seconds you can find out how many members say "Jimmy Buffet" is their favorite singer, or "Antiques Roadshow" is their favorite TV show, or "chicken curry" is a favorite meal. You can zap a message to any of these folks, or you can quickly locate members in your ZIP code who are science-fiction buffs. MySpace as a research tool can produce the same results as an expensive, traditional direct mail campaign—and it's free.

Making friends on MySpace

There are several ways to find people on MySpace who might be in your target market—by searching for *tennis, self-improvement, organic food,* or whatever field you're in. Once you've found potential friends, you can send a request for them to "add" you as a friend. The invitee can accept, decline, or ignore your request, although most people accept.

Once you're friends with someone on MySpace, you can post comments on each other's profile pages and see each other's full circle of friends. Here's how to find friends and potential readership on MySpace:

• **Browse friends lists of members interested in your field.** Find the MySpace profiles of similar businesses and target market as yours. On the right side, scroll down a bit to the link See All of [Name]'s Friends. Start sending invitations—you'll get many potential customers this way. Here's another twist: Send an invitation to a famous business operator, and if they accept, post a comment, which appears on the bottom right of their MySpace page. More exposure for you.

• **Search.** Click Search on the top toolbar on the MySpace home page. You can limit your search to certain areas such as Blogs, Music Interest, Books Interest, or others. Let's imagine you're looking for MySpace members interested in organic food. Click on Search and enter "organic food." Presto, you've got a list of every MySpace member who's used the words "organic food" in that part of their profile. Also, use the **Affiliations for Networking** search tool a bit farther down the page.

• **Browse for friends.** If your business serves a local clientele, it's useful to browse for potential MySpace friends by geographic area. On the home page, click Browse and the **Advanced** tab. You'll be able to view member profiles within a specified distance of postal ZIP codes, as well as other criteria such as age, gender, religion, and income. Many single MySpace members use this function to scout potential dates, but it's useful for entrepreneurs who are advertising a local business on MySpace.

- **Browse comments on other member profiles.** Comments from MySpace friends appear on the bottom right of profile pages. The most recent comments appear at the top, accompanied by the comment writer's photo or image. Members who leave these comments tend to be the most active and vocal MySpace users, and make good friends. In particular, seek out people who've posted thoughtful comments, like "Enjoyed seeing your profile and getting more information." Skip messages such as, "You ROCK, Man!!!"

- **Sending friends requests.** Once you find a potential friend, click <u>Add to Friends</u> under their profile's main photo on the left. And if you want to increase the odds of making a real connection, don't stop there—send a personalized message by clicking the <u>Send a Message</u> link. It requires some extra work, but you can't convert "friends" into customers simply by pecking on your mouse button.

- **Accepting friends.** Once you've done some networking on MySpace, people will start seeking you out. But don't feel obligated to accept anyone and everyone. Click to their profile page first, and make sure their interests are in line with yours.

There are two ways of approaching MySpace friendships: trying to acquire as big a list as possible, or having a smaller group you can make stronger connections with individually. In any case, the people who ultimately will become a customer will be those in your core groups, those who feel a connection.

- **Create an "event."** Launching a new product or opening a new branch office? Throw a party and announce it to your MySpace friends by creating a MySpace event and sending invitations. To get started, simply click <u>Events</u> on the top navigation bar on any MySpace page, then <u>Create New Event</u>.

Leaving comments. After you become someone's MySpace friend, visit their profile and add a comment. This is an effective networking tool—not only will your new friend read your comment, but people who visit your friend's page will see it, too. Avoid the most overused MySpace comment: "Thanks for the add," which is short-hand for "thanks for adding me as a friend." It's a cliché, and a missed opportunity. Take a moment to think of a meaningful comment, based on something about your new friend's profile, like "Hey, my favorite author is Hemingway, too!"

Sending messages. MySpace has an internal e-mail system and an instant-messaging system for sending private notes. You can include your regular e-mail signature, including links and photos. But if the message isn't too personal, you're better off posting your thoughts publicly, as a "comment" on your friend's page. This increases your visibility on MySpace, making it that much easier for new friends and readers to discover you.

Responding to messages. When you receive a MySpace message, you'll receive an alert at the e-mail address you used to register at MySpace. To network effectively, respond promptly to your messages. If someone makes the effort to write to you, they'll be waiting for a response. Don't alienate potential friends by letting messages pile up unanswered.

Sending personal replies is time-consuming and you won't see instant results. But remember, the personal connection you provide with a thoughtful reply is something readers will remember. These are the folks who will feel good about you and recommend you to others. Marketing experts call these people "influencers" because once you've made a good impression on them, they tell their friends, and this word-of-mouth process is amplified and accelerated on the Internet. Contacting these influencers is your key to making your business stand out amid the clutter and noise on the Web.

Sending bulletins. Once you've built a network of MySpace friends, the ability to send them MySpace bulletins is a powerful tool. Your bulletin won't be e-mailed like your personal messages are, but the headlines will appear on all your friends' "bulletin board" area. Whether you have two dozen MySpace friends or 20,000, the ability to let them all know about a new product or offer simultaneously is a unique tool.

To post a bulletin, click the Post bulletin link in the box labeled **My Mail**.

Like personal messages, bulletins are a feature you'll want to use sparingly, to preserve their impact. If you bombard friends with frequent bulletins that aren't compelling, they'll start ignoring them, and perhaps be irritated enough to drop you as a friend.

Here are the kinds of noteworthy events you'll want to send bulletins about:

• Your new product becomes available for sale at retailers or on your Web site.

- You get profiled in a national newspaper or magazine.

- You've won a prestigious award.

- You've just been booked to appear on *The Oprah Winfrey Show* or *Larry King Live*.

Picking your 'Top 8'

After you've explored MySpace a bit, you'll notice under each member's **About Me** section are pictures of eight friends, along with a link to that member's complete friends list. By default, the eight pictures displayed are the first eight friends added by that member, known in MySpace parlance as the Top 8.

You can shuffle your Top 8 to add zing to your profile page. Take your most influential or well-known friends and move them to the front by scrolling down to the box labeled **My Friend Space** and clicking Change my Top Friends. Seek out more authors or experts in your field, and request they add you as a friend. Move them into your Top 8, too. This is a valuable cross-promotion tool because it boosts your exposure among members who are in your target market.

If you're really popular on MySpace, don't limit yourself to just eight top friends. Click Change my Top Friends, and on the top left corner of the screen you'll see a drop-down menu where you can increase the number of Top Friends displayed on your main page to as many as 40. If you'd rather display fewer Top Friends, you can reduce it to four.

Author Marcy Dermansky creatively used her MySpace Top 8 to help promote her debut novel *Twins*. Drawing from her 3,000 MySpace friends, Dermansky found several with names matching the character names in her book, like Lauren, Chloe and Smita. She moved them to her Top 8. For the more unusual names in the book, like Jürgen and Yumiko, she had to search for new friends using MySpace's search engine. New friends who got invitations were so intrigued about the book, they often bought it simply to read about namesake characters, adding to the book's buzz. See:

www.MySpace.com/ChloeAndSue

Tips for working MySpace

After you've signed up at MySpace, pay special attention to these elements of your profile:

Headline. When you set up your MySpace account, you're able to upload a picture—perhaps your portrait or an image of your store or leading product—and a short message labeled your **headline**. Use this space to identify yourself and your business: who you are, and what you do. Use this to its maximum effect. You can update this section anytime.

About Me. Here, list your history and your influences. HTML is allowed in this section, so include prominent links to your own Web site or blog.

Photos. Whether you use a photo of yourself, your company's logo or an image of a product, use professional photos and artwork when possible. Hire a real photographer or enlist a talented friend with a digital camera. Don't brand yourself an amateur by using a crummy snapshot.

Your MySpace blog

As a MySpace member you're able to publish a blog linked to your profile. Here you can include content too lengthy for your messages or bulletins. Blog posts are searchable through MySpace and regular search engines like Google, so naturally you'll want to include plenty of information about your business.

If you're already publishing a blog on your own domain, you don't necessarily have to reinvent the wheel on your MySpace blog. Simply repurpose some earlier content from your own blog, posting it on your MySpace blog for the benefit of your new friends.

Ask your friends to "subscribe" to your blog by clicking Subscribe to this Blog while they're visiting. Then they'll receive e-mail alerts of your new posts.

To add a post to your blog, click Manage Blog from the menu just to the right of your main profile picture, then scroll down to the box labeled **My Controls** and click Post New Blog.

User-generated content

Contests and giveaways are reliable ways to promote products on MySpace too, the only limit is your imagination. Offer a monthly drawing for a free product or service, awarded to one of your new friends. Just the act of offering a free product will encourage others to buy it—they won't want to wait to see if they've won the contest. However, don't go overboard with expensive prizes, and don't call what you're doing a "sweepstakes," since this is against MySpace's participation agreement.

Your most enthusiastic customers can end up providing your best marketing ideas. For example, in 2007 Doritos said its Super Bowl commercial was produced by a consumer with a budget of $12. Doritos had invited the public to create 30-second commercials, with the winning video being aired during the game. Fans submitted 1,020 videos and Doritos awarded $10,000 to five finalists.

MySpace Groups

Joining various MySpace "groups" is perhaps the best way to find new friends. From MySpace.com, click Groups on the top navigation bar. On the left, you'll see a link for Search Groups, where you can search for your topic area. For example, if your company sells automobile accessories, you'll want to join the "MySpace Automotive Group" and the "Classic Collector and Muscle Group," among others. You can search for groups by keyword or browse by broad categories, such as "Fashion & Style" and "Pets & Animals." The groups with the most members will be listed on top.

Joining groups is a better way to connect with potential customers than just randomly sending friend invitations to any profile that you happen to see. Some groups allow you to post bulletins where you can mention your business or product. But check on this: It's important to know the group's terms of use, and you don't want to be accused of spamming the group.

If you're lucky one of your customers might start a MySpace group about your company. One of the biggest success stories on MySpace, for example, is Wawa, the eastern convenience-store chain. Its MySpace "I love Wawa" group has 6,500 members who trade stories and "claim" their favorite store location.

Interests. Here's where members enter their basic likes, in categories such as books, music, movies, television, and others. Don't leave this blank. This is how many people will find you on MySpace, by searching for friends who have common interests.

Create your own group

You can create your own MySpace group, giving members several more avenues to discover you. You can attract a wider readership by forming a group dedicated to your business or mission. And by doing a good job of running the show, you'll establish your credibility as an expert in your field.

To create a MySpace group, from the main Groups page, click <u>Create Group</u>.

If you already have a big, dedicated following, you can make it all about you, starting a fan club Group for yourself on MySpace. Or you can enlist one of your friends to do it.

Uploading videos

Video is a great way to promote yourself and your work on MySpace. People respond more when they can associate a face and a voice with the rest of your presentation.

Lots of new companies have popped up recently to provide online video content to promote your business. If you don't have the resources to hire a video producer, it's fairly easy to create your own video. A simple question-and-answer session can provide video content to publicize your business. Position yourself in a chair in front of a bookshelf or potted plant and have an interviewer ask a series of questions about your business. If you're on a budget but aren't able to shoot your own video, solicit volunteer film students from a local college. Students are usually willing to work on such projects, which provide experience and something to show on their resumes.

MySpace best practices

And here are several more rules of thumb for using MySpace as a publicity tool, and you can apply these same principles to most other social-networking sits:

- **It's better to give than receive.** Don't give the hard-sell. Social networking is all about communication and providing valuable information that will draw others to you. Be generous and you'll be richer.

- **Try to keep your MySpace pages streamlined and clutter-free.** Make sure that anyone who sees it can easily discover your business.

- **Focus on your target market.** Don't get side-tracked marketing to millions of people who aren't the right fit for your product or service—you'll quickly get overwhelmed. You'll waste time communicating with people who aren't going to be interested.

- **If you're advertising a local business, be sure to include your city on your display name.** You'll improve your response because your city name will catch the eye of the people in your region.

- **Have a signup form to capture e-mail addresses.** An opt-in list of prospects will become more valuable the larger it grows. To encourage signups, offer a widget, newsletter, coupon or some other incentive.

- **Offer a syndication code to help friends spread the word about your site.** Offer the code for a banner ad or "widget" so friends can link to your site from their MySpace page.

- **Link to your own Web site.** Briefly describe the benefits visitors will find there.

- **Keep your name in front of people by posting frequently to your MySpace blog and by sending a bulletin of the blog entry to all your friends.** But don't abuse the privilege—if you post too frequently without something of value, your friends will quickly decide to ignore you, or delete you from their list of friends.

- **Don't send unsolicited messages to MySpace users.** The message will either be ignored or the user will report it as spam, perhaps prompting MySpace to disable or delete your account.

- **Don't use corporate mumbo-jumbo.** Write and speak as if you're with a friend.

- **Don't send more than 400 friend requests in a single day.** MySpace monitors usage of your account and can restrict your privileges or even delete your account. Don't use scripts or software robots to send friend requests because this can prompt MySpace to disable your account.

- **Don't feel obligated to accept every friend who zaps an invitation your way.** It's best to concentrate on having 50 friends you truly connect with, rather than having thousands of friends you quickly forget about.

- **To leverage MySpace as a professional asset, your page must look professional.** Your potential friends will check out your existing friends, so your MySpace utility will be undermined by having too many friends who have no connection to your niche. It's fine to have some oddballs in there, but be certain you have a clear connection with your Top 8 friends.

- **To keep the hits coming, you've got to maintain your MySpace page.** Throwing together a page and never visiting or tweaking it will do little good.

- **Don't promote your MySpace profile at the expense of your own domain.** MySpace is a great networking tool, but you don't want to depend on it exclusively. Perhaps someday MySpace will go out of business, begin charging high fees, or simply won't fit your image anymore. In any case, you can purchase an important insurance policy for only $9 a year by registering your own domain name and forwarding the traffic to your MySpace page—your domain registrar can handle this for you. Instead of printing your MySpace URL in your sales literature or on business cards, print your own domain, and you can forward the traffic to MySpace if you wish. Later, if you decide to focus your efforts elsewhere, you can take your traffic with you by forwarding it someplace else.

MySpace best practices

Like other Web sites, MySpace has a Terms of Service document that outlines what is allowed and prohibited on the site. Among other things, MySpace outlaws these activities:

- "Commercial" use of the site, such as harvesting names or contact information in order to send unsolicited commercial messages.

- Publishing physical contact information such as phone numbers, street addresses, and e-mail addresses.

- Posting content deemed " offensive, illegal or violate the rights, harm, or threaten the safety of any person."

See the full MySpace Terms of Service here:

www.myspace.com/Modules/Common/Pages/ TermsConditions.aspx

Time-saving tips for MySpace

By default, MySpace sends you e-mail notifications whenever you receive new messages, comments, blog comments, or new friend requests. Once your friend list exceeds a few hundred people, you can save time by turning off these automated alerts and simply managing your profile by logging into MySpace once a day.

To stop MySpace's automated e-mails, go to MySpace.com and click "Account Settings." Check the box labeled "Do not send me notification emails," then click the "Change" button at the bottom of the page.

You can also save time by delegating certain MySpace administrative tasks to an assistant or colleague, such as:

- Locating potential new "friends" and sending invitations.

- Posting prewritten materials to your MySpace blog.

- Screening incoming friend requests and, when appropriate, approving them.

However, you should appoint a single individual within your organization to engage with the community of MySpace and other sites where you're participating. This helps ensure you project a consistent message.

Customizing MySpace

Once you have mastered the basics of MySpace, you may want to further customize your profile by adjusting the background colors and text sizes and placements. You can alter the appearance of various elements of your profile by going to MySpace.com and clicking <u>Edit Profile</u>, and inserting HTML (HyperText Markup Language) code into most of the portions of your profile where you've entered text. For example, to make a word in your profile appear in bold text, you'd insert the opening tag **\<b\>** before the word, and after the word you'd use the closing tag, **\</b\>**. Other tags can be used to change the size, color, and position of your text, or to add pictures and other graphical elements. To see a list of HTML tags, see this reference site:

www.htmlquick.com/reference/tags.html

For more ideas on customizing your profile with more elaborate layout tools, see this reference site:

www.pimp-my-profile.com

Additionally, if your profile is related to a performing arts business, you'll have some additional options—you can open a dedicated "music" or "comedy" MySpace profile. Click the "music" or "comedy" tab from any MySpace page, then click "artist signup." Just like a personal page, music and comedy profiles are free. The layout is slightly different, and has a few extra bells and whistles, depending on whether you have recorded music or videos and lists of upcoming appearances.

MySpace advertising opportunities

Companies with larger marketing budgets can consider a sponsored branded profile, for which MySpace charges about $35,000. This removes the standard advertising banner that occupies the top portion of regular MySpace profiles, and adds optional functions such as customized games, voting, quizzes and contests. MySpace also helps drive traffic to these custom profiles according to the demographic information it has about members.

MySpace is just one of a growing number of social-networking sites. Amazon.com is an investor in **www.43Things.com**, which was founded by some ex-Amazon employees. On 43Things, members list goals, things they want to accomplish, and assign tags to help put them in touch with like-minded members.

More social-networking sites

This sector of the Internet is growing and changing at a terrific rate, and bears watching. It's entirely possible that MySpace won't continue its overwhelming domination of Internet social networking indefinitely. Already, niche social networks are emerging, splintering audiences into narrower interests. Someday an entrepreneur will launch the "MySpace" of woodworking, scuba diving, or auto restoration. Be on the lookout for up-and-coming networks in your sphere. Or perhaps you'll have an idea for launching a network yourself.

Here are other leading social networking sites. You can navigate to each of these sites by adding a **.com** to the end of the names:

LinkedIn, known as a business-to-business social network, helps professionals find and contact one another to find new jobs or leads by referral only. LinkedIn has no chat rooms or discussion boards, and personal profiles have no photos.

Facebook made its name by serving college students who wanted to network with other students at their campus. More than 80 percent of students who attend U.S. colleges have a profile, according to one survey. In 2006 Facebook began accepting non-students, and now has many members from the business community, military and other sectors.

Gather caters to middle-aged users, and is backed by public radio's American Public Media Group. Unlike most other networks, Gather advertises on television to lure new members, then pays members for submitting content to the site.

SecondLife is a three-dimensional virtual world in which users interact with one another using avatars. Second Life is growing quickly and could popularize the idea of avatar-based marketing.

YouTube is a video sharing site purchased by Google in 2006. It's believed to be the second most-popular social networking site behind MySpace.

Classmates allows members to keep in touch with high school and college classmates. Unlike most other networks, members must pay a fee to access other profiles and contact friends.

Flickr is a social network for sharing photos, although photos can also be made private. Users can tag their photos with keywords which enables others to search for them.

Xanga emphasizes blogs, and allows members to enhance their profiles with special features by paying a fee.

Orkut, owned by Google, has not been marketed extensively as of mid-2007 but someday may benefit greatly from its connection to the search engine giant.

Bebo is especially popular among young adults, with an average user age of about 20 years. Users can add home-made polls and quizzes to their profile.

Friendster was one of the early popular social networking sites and has more than 30 million active users. Users create profiles and add music and video clips and blogs. The site is a little less flexible than MySpace, which overtook it in 2004 as the most popular.

The company Ning hosts a free, easy-to-use Web platform enabling anyone to create their own social network, and more than 60,000 people have already done so. At **www.Ning.com**, you can create a customized social network by choosing a combination of features, including blogs, photos and forums. You can add your brand logo, then invite friends and customers to create their own personal profile pages on your network.

What attracts many business operators to Ning is the element of control. Unlike MySpace, where customers might be lured away by advertising for competing products and services, Ning allows the creator of a social network to administer membership, content and advertising.

Ning earns a profit by displaying advertisements along the right hand side of every page. You can eliminate the ads by paying Ning $19.95 per month. Ning allows you to use your own domain name instead of a Ning address for an additional $4.95 per month.

Getting buzz on social networks

No matter which of the social networks you use, there are broad principles you can apply to each to attract attention and maximize your effectiveness.

• Complete your profile completely wherever appropriate. List all your products, services, qualifications, specialties, partners, and so on. Many people will find you by conducting a keyword search on the social network or at Google.com, so make sure you've seeded your profile with all the relevant details.

• Include testimonials from happy customers or well-known people in your field. Anyone can have a profile on a social network, but the ones that are taken seriously have credible people vouching for their trustworthiness.

• Have the largest number of friends possible within your target market. The more complete your list, the better the odds that new people in your target market will discover you promptly.

Building your Web site

Few people can benefit more from a Web site than a business owner. A simple do-it-yourself site can provide a huge visibility boost at very low cost. Even if you are active on social networking sites, it's essential to maintain a Web site or blog that serves as your online home base.

Before you begin planning your site, consider your target audience and what type of information you want to give them. Whatever your approach, the goal is to provide content your target audience finds worthwhile.

Getting involved

Many small-business owners outsource their Web project, paying a designer $500 or more to build what amounts to an online brochure. That's a big mistake, because static Web sites with little content don't draw the repeat traffic that will bring you new business.

Although it may seem like a daunting technical challenge, building your own site is easier than ever, thanks to improved software tools. Every major Internet hosting company now offers a variety of design templates you can use to start quickly, without having to learn computer coding. You'll gain much more from your Web site if it's maintained by you or a close associate.

Three basic options exist for those establishing their first site:

• **Do it yourself** by registering a domain name and building your own site. This option requires you to learn a few software tools, but provides more flexibility and control. **GoDaddy.com** offers fast, reliable service, and a wide variety of Web domain registration and hosting plans at competitive prices. There's no setup fee and no annual commitment is required. GoDaddy's economy plan includes 5 gigabytes of disk space, 500 e-mail accounts, forums, blogging, and photo galleries for $3.99 a month. This hosting company and most competitors such as **www.Register.com** offer simple tools and templates for building your own site.

• **Using a free account** at a network such as MySpace.com, Google Pages, Blogger.com, or LiveJournal.com. A packaged solution like this is easy to learn, but provides less flexibility. Some sites feature advertising you can't control, which can distract visitors from your message.

• **Consult a Web designer** through your local Yellow Pages, or an online firm that specializes in designing business sites.

One way to get started quickly while preserving your future options is to pay GoDaddy or another registrar $9 to register your own domain name, such as **www.YourName.com**, then forwarding the traffic to your account at MySpace, Blogger, or others. Later, if you choose to build a dedicated site, you can forward the traffic there. This strategy allows you to start building your online audience without the risk of losing readers if you switch your focus to another site.

In any case, it's prudent to make backup copies of all content you post to a free account on sites like Blogger or MySpace, since these free accounts are sometimes deleted accidentally.

Google Pages is an easy, free tool you can use to create Web pages quickly without having to learn HTML code. Google will host up to 100 megabytes of Web pages at no charge. Open an account at **www.Pages.Google.com**.

Your domain

If you're committed to actively supporting your business online, it's best to stake out your own territory on the Web. This means registering your own domain name, which you alone control. GoDaddy.com, Register.com and NetworkSolutions.com are well known, reliable firms where you can buy a package of services—domain registration, Web hosting and e-mail accounts.

You may want to use the name of your business as the domain. Or you may want to use the name of a product, registering a domain for each product. Keep your domain name short and memorable so people who see it or hear of it can recall it. Hyphenated domain names are usually a bad idea—they're harder to remember and they fail the "radio test" because they're difficult to repeat in conversation.

Building blocks of your site

The great thing about a Web site is you can always add to it. Here are some basic elements you'll want to consider adding to your site:

- Content. Nobody will visit a site that's merely an advertisement. Your content can be a series of articles, white papers, case studies, or even feedback from your readers.

- Your biography or a history of your company.

- Links to purchase your products, either on your site or online retailers. The more choices you offer buyers, the better.

- Reviews of your products or services.

- A form where visitors can enter their e-mail address to subscribe to a newsletter or site updates.

- Contact information—your e-mail address (or a form that forwards messages) and perhaps postal address and phone number.

- A "media room" with any press releases announcing your products or any news coverage.

Waiting for results

Building a Web site can be a lonely process. Don't expect a big response in the first month or even the next six months. Often it takes an entire year for a Web site or blog to gain momentum. But if you concentrate on producing a useful site with quality content, word will get around.

As you build your site, keep one general idea in mind: Unless you're already a superstar or your business is well known, don't make your Web site about *you*. Make it about *your visitor*. Provide compelling content that solves problems, entertains, sparks curiosity, or inspires. Everything else will follow.

Resist the temptation to pack your site with fancy features like flashy graphics or voices or music that plays automatically. Usually these doodads have the opposite effect than what was intended—they make your site slow, irritating, noisy and hard to read.

Blogging for business

Julie Powell moved to New York to become an actress. A few years later, she realized she was 30 years old, working a dead-end job to pay the bills, and still had no acting prospects. Then, on a visit to Texas, she borrowed her mother's copy of Julia Child's landmark 1961 cookbook, *Mastering the Art of French Cooking, Volume 1.* Back in her cramped kitchen on Long Island, Powell cooked one of the recipes for her husband, who enjoyed it so much he urged her to attend culinary school and become a professional cook.

Instead, Powell decided to teach herself, and let the whole world watch. She vowed to cook each of the book's 524 recipes during the following year, and write a diary about it on a Web log, or *blog*. Powell wrote about killing lobsters, boiling calves hooves, and making homemade mayonnaise, but she didn't confine herself to cooking. For good measure, she heaped on details of her sex life, recipes for reviving a romance, and snide remarks about her backstabbing coworkers.

As Powell began one entry: "My husband almost divorced me last night, and it was all because of the sauce tartar." Her storytelling was so good, word got around fast and thousands began reading her blog—regardless of whether they cared about French cuisine. A write-up in the *New York Times* brought thousands more readers.

By the time Powell was winding down her project, publishers were knocking on the door with book contracts, and her blog turned into the bestseller *Julie and Julia: 365 Days, 524 Recipes, 1 Tiny Apartment Kitchen*. More than 100,000 copies sold its first year, a monster success for any memoir, let alone a book by an unknown, chronically unemployed actress.

Here's a humorous online trailer featuring Powell chatting about the book and how it happened:

www.Blip.tv/file/78726

Blogging is a relatively easy way for you to publicize your business and even improve your writing while you're at it. If you can write an e-mail, you can write a blog—it's the easiest, cheapest, and perhaps best way for authors to find an audience and connect with customers. Blogging is an informal, intimate form of communication that inspires trust among your readers.

For the same reasons that traditional advertising is less effective than ever, a blog can be highly effective for promoting your business. People interested in your topic seek out your message.

What is a blog?

Put simply, a blog is a Web site with a few interactive features. You don't have to call it a blog unless you want to. It's possible that within a few years, nearly every Web site will have interactive features, and people simply won't call them blogs anymore.

You needn't know anything about computers to blog. Simply type into a form, and presto—the whole world can see it. Your blog is a *content management* system—a painless way to build and maintain a platform where readers can discover and enjoy your writing.

Who blogs? Every company approaches it differently. Sometimes a chief executive or a marketing department leads the charge. Some blogs are company-wide blogs, and anyone can contribute. In other cases there are individual blogs for senior executives or sections of a company.

A blog can be a part of your Web site, or it can be *the* Web site. The main thing that distinguishes a blog from a plain old Web site is that a blog is frequently updated with short messages, or *posts*. Readers often chime in with their own comments at the bottom of each post. This free exchange of ideas is what makes blogs a revolutionary tool for entrepreneurs: A successful blog is a constant stream of ideas, inspiration, perspective, and advice—it's a real-time, global focus group.

Why blogs are better

Some business owners who already have a Web site resist the idea of blogging and the "extra work" it entails. Their reasoning is, "Why create more work?" Well, blogging can help you maximize the effectiveness of things you're probably already doing, like answering e-mails from your customers.

Compared with other types of Internet publicity content such as static Web sites or e-mail newsletters, blogs provide three big advantages:

• Blogs are easy to start and maintain.

• The short, serialized content of blogs encourages regular readership, repeated exposure to your products or services.

- Blogs rank high in search-engine results from Google and other providers, making them easy to find.

Why do blogs get so much traffic from search engines? First, blogs are topical. When you're writing about the same topics and ideas day in and day out, your site becomes packed with the keywords your target market is searching for. Stay at it awhile, and it becomes nearly impossible for your likely customers to miss you, thanks to Google and the other search engines. Most new visitors will find your site by using a search engine, after looking for words and topics contained in your Web pages.

Another reason blogs are so easy to find is that search engines usually rank them higher than other types of Web sites. Thus your links can show up at the top of search results, which is where most people click.

Google and the other search engines give extra credit to blogs for a couple of reasons:

- Blogs are updated frequently, and the assumption is "fresh" content is more valuable.

- Blogs tend to have many links from other Web pages with similar content. The assumption is that because other bloggers and Webmasters have decided to link to your content, it's probably valuable.

Your visibility in search results is key, since about 40 percent of your new visitors will likely arrive via a Web search. If your site ranks highly in Web searches for the keywords related to your book, you'll have a constant source of well-qualified visitors and new customers.

Breathing the blogosphere

Step 1 in becoming a blogger is to consume some blogs yourself. Reading other blogs gives you a quick feel for what works, what doesn't, and the techniques you'll want to apply to your own blog.

There are millions of blogs, and finding ones that suit you can be like searching for a needle in a haystack. There's no easy way to filter out low-quality blogs—you've just got to sample what's out there.

A good place to begin is by browsing for blogs about your hobbies, pastimes and passions. You can find a list of the most popular blogs here:

www.Technorati.com/pop/blogs

You can drill down into niche territory by browsing **www.Technorati.com/blogs**, where you'll find a menu of subjects on the left. You can also search blogs by keyword at these sites:

www.Blogsearch.Google.com
www.Feedster.com
www.IceRocket.com

Once you've found a few blogs of interest, it's easy to find more. Bloggers tend to link to one another, both within their blog posts, and often within a side menu of links known as a *blogroll*.

A handy tool for keeping track of all your blogs is a *newsreader* or *aggregator*, which saves you the trouble of poking around the Web, looking for new blog posts. Instead, your newsreader gathers and displays updates for you. One free, easy-to-use reader is:

www.Bloglines.com

You'll quickly learn which blogs you've subscribed to are must-reads, and which can be ignored or deleted.

Connecting with readers

It's natural to be apprehensive about starting a blog. When you first begin, it may feel like being on stage without a script or a view of the audience. Don't worry, feedback will come soon enough. Remember, there's no right or wrong way to blog. The only rule is your target audience must find something worthwhile.

One way to ease into blogging is to start with a temporary blog at **www.Blogger.com**, where you can set up a free practice blog in five minutes. Take a dry run for a week or two, then make your blog public when you're ready.

A lively blog is like a free focus group: It provides you with constant feedback, criticism and new ideas. Your blog readers will pepper you with comments and e-mails.

Indeed, the true power of blogging is the momentum created by your audience. Once your blog has 100 frequent readers, it has critical mass. It may take six months or a year to get there, but from there it's all downhill. Members of your core audience begin competing to hand you the most useful, compelling ideas by writing comments on your blog and e-mailing you directly. That's when your blog becomes electric, a magnet attracting new visitors. Your core audience swells as word of mouth goes viral.

Blog comments: pros and cons

Most blogs include space below the author's posts for readers to add their own views. These comments can take the conversation in a totally new direction, and become the most interesting material on your blog, thanks purely to your readers' efforts.

For the blogger, comments bring three key benefits:

• Instant feedback on your content, and a sense of what your audience finds valuable.

• Feeling of participation and loyalty among your audience.

• Adding valuable keyword density to your site, making it much more visible in search-engine results.

Like any tool, however, comments can be abused. It's not unusual to see rude or off-topic comments on some blogs, and even "spam comments" written solely to plant links back to the spammer's site. The worst spammers even use software robots, which scour the Web for target blogs and insert their junk links. Spam comments are usually along the lines of, "Hey, great blog. Come see us at **www.Cheap-Viagra.com.**"

Fortunately, most problem comments can be prevented by using countermeasures like *comment moderation*: you review and approve new comments before they appear on your blog. Another option is to allow readers to post comments immediately, and you review them later. The advantage is your readers get immediate gratification in seeing their comments posted as they submit them.

Most spam comments can be prevented by using *word verification*, requiring comment writers to type a short series of characters displayed in an image. This stops spam comments from software robots. The technical term is CAPTCHA, which stands for "Completely Automated Public Turing test to tell Computers and Humans Apart."

Blog style

Just as every business is unique, there's an endless variety of blog styles and flavors. All the blogging services have page templates, allowing you to start with a basic design and add a few personal elements.

Don't get bogged down looking for the "perfect" design. You'll always be free to tweak your design later, or do a complete overhaul. The most important thing is to get started adding content and building your audience.

The main design requirement is readability. Plain vanilla blogs are fine, and are actually preferred by most readers—it's the words that count. Black text on a white background might seem uninspired, but it's much easier on the eyes than white text on a black background or some other color. A plain masthead, simply your blog title in capital letters, is fine to start. The important thing is to get started.

Your blog's angle

A business blog can approach its topic from several directions:

- New developments.

- New products or services.

- Hot-button issues of the day.

- What other blogs or media are saying.

You can publish a blog in the style of a perpetual newsletter, an aggregation of interesting tidbits about your business or the interests of your customers. As you notice new things and write about them, each post is stacked on top, and with each new post added on top, one of the older posts is bumped from the bottom and sent to your archives.

Let's imagine you're writing a blog on the topic of *Organic Gardening*. Your blog could serve as an information clearinghouse covering every conceivable angle and trend of organic good growing, cooking and consuming. You'll constantly monitor consumer and trade media for the latest news on organic growing, interpret this material for your audience, and link to the source material, adding your own commentary.

Your blog could include:

• Questions from your blog readers on organic fruit and vegetables, along with your answers.

• Guest articles from experts on organic gardening.

• New books and magazines on the topic.

• Meal recipes.

• Maps of the best places to grow organic food.

• Listings and maps of markets offering organic food.

• Reviews of cookbooks addressing natural, organic, fruit and dessert preparation.

Raw materials for posts

A free, easy way to find new raw material for your blog is to create a *Google Alert*, which will automatically scour thousands of media sources for any keywords you specify. You'll be alerted via e-mail when something containing your keywords appears in newspapers, magazines, Web sites, or other sources. Sign up at:

www.Google.com/alerts

Google Alerts are also a handy way to monitor mentions of your blog title, your name, the name of your business and competitors.

Your blog's title

A blog title usually spans the top portion of each page like a newspaper masthead. Titles are usually short and catchy—perhaps just a couple of nonsense words like *Boing Boing*, or a made-up compound word like *Rocket-Boom* or *BuzzMachine*. The name could be a non sequitur or double-entendre like PostSecret. Sometimes a title is just a title, like *The Official Google Weblog*.

Try to include in your title the most critical keyword related to your niche. *Joe's Organic Strawberry Growing, Baking and Eating Guide* is a good title. A poor title would be *Joe's Thoughts and Ideas about Fruit* because nobody would search for something like that, and if they saw it, they couldn't guess what it's about. Be obvious. Pick a few words that will be easy for people to remember and to repeat in conversation and e-mails.

Writing your blog posts

The essential ingredient of a blog is its short entries, or posts. They're arranged in reverse chronological order, with the newest at top. Posts can be a few sentences long, or many paragraphs long, and often link to outside information like blogs, newspaper stories, or multimedia clips hosted elsewhere on the Web.

Nearly any tidbit of information relevant to your audience can be spun into a blog post of some type:

- **Informational.** A news-oriented blurb. A new development.

- **Question/Answer.** Easy to write, and fun to read. Reliable material, even if you have to make up the question.

- **Instructional.** Can be a longer post, a tutorial that explains how to do something related to your niche.

- **Link posts.** Find an interesting blog post elsewhere. Link to it and add your own spin.

- **Rant.** Let off some steam, and let it rip. Interesting blogs don't play it safe, they take sides.

- **Book review.** Review a book related to your field. It can be a new book or a classic that newcomers haven't heard of.

- **Product reviews.** The word "review" is a popular search term. Give your frank opinion, and encourage your readers to chime in with their own views.

- **Lists.** Write about the "Top 5 Ways" to do a task, or the "Top 10 Reasons" for such-and-such. Readers love lists. If someone else publishes a list, you can summarize it or critique it on your own blog.

- **Interviews.** Chat with someone in your field. Provide a text summary on your blog. You can also add a transcript or even an audio file.

- **Case studies.** Report on how so-and-so does such-and-such. You don't have to call it a "case study," just tell the story.

- **Profiles.** Profiles focus on a particular person, a personality. The person profiled can be someone well known in your field, or perhaps a newcomer nobody's heard of.

Most blogs are conversational and informal, but that doesn't provide a license to be sloppy. You want your blog to reflect favorably on your business, and that requires attention to detail—not to mention beginning your sentences with capital letters and ending them with periods. It's worth proofreading and spell-checking your posts before publishing. Keeping your paragraphs short will minimize your rewriting chores.

One helpful feature for you and your readers is blog categories. Assign each post to one or more categories, such as "technology," "marketing," "features," "reviews," or however you can best divide your material. Category headings can be listed on your blog's margin, and are especially valuable for new readers.

Over the long haul

Blogs evolve, and priorities change. It's impossible to draw up a road map for the future, but here are some strategic ideas to help give your blog long-term direction:

• **Write an *anchor* post every month or two.** An anchor post is a tutorial-style piece that teaches your readers how to do something, like *How to Pick Fruit at its Peak of Flavor* or *Top 10 Ways to Prevent Identity Theft*. It can be the length of a short magazine article, perhaps 750 to 1,500 words. This type of content is evergreen—it won't become obsolete, and you can continually refer back to it in your subsequent posts. Every month or two, add another anchor post.

• **Write at least one new post a day.** Frequent posting keeps your audience interested and jogs your creativity. The more you post, the more you'll be picked up by the search engines, and the more new people will find your blog, become regular readers. The first two sentences are the hardest of a post, and it's all downhill after that.

- **Comment on other blogs in your niche.** This will attract fellow bloggers and their readers who follow the link in your comment back to your blog. Make a meaningful comment that advances the discussion, don't just say "I agree."

- **Link to other blogs from within your blog posts.** With certain blogging software, this is known as a *trackback*, and leaves a summary of your blog post on the original blog. Result: More bloggers and readers find you.

- **Ask for comments on your blog.** End your posts with a question, prompting your readers for feedback. When practical, end your posts with a question like, "What do you think?", or "What's your take on this?" Readers are often more interested in what *they* have to say than in what *you* have to say.

- **Don't write when you're angry.** If you're upset, cool off for a few hours—or a day—before posting something nasty that you might regret later. It's nearly impossible to delete stuff on the Web. You might erase something from your blog, but the text can be archived in dozens of other places.

- **Link to your old content.** After you've been blogging for a while, you'll have five or six previous blog posts that were most popular with readers—drawing lots of links, traffic and comments. For the benefit of new readers, link to these previous posts when you write about the same topics in the future. Add a small menu of these posts on the sidebar of your blog, with a heading such as **Lively Conversations** or **Greatest Hits**.

- **Add artwork.** Sprinkling stock photos and illustrations in your blog posts is a simple way to add visual appeal. Images are eyeball magnets. Writing a post about how to fix a flat tire? Include a small stock photo of someone installing a tire. The site **www.sxc.hu** has thousands of royalty-free photos you can search by keyword. You needn't illustrate your posts literally, which can get boring. Let's imagine your post concerns some type of *manipulation*. It's the key idea and the main word in your post title. How could you illustrate it? Just search for "manipulation" at the photo site mentioned above, and you'll see dozens of images you could use as a smart illustration—like photos of puppets, marionettes or chess pawns. If your first keyword doesn't find results, try a synonym—or if you're feeling ironic, try an antonym.

- **Create an RSS or Atom feed.** Be sure your blog automatically posts a feed, so readers who use an aggregator like Bloglines can read this way if they wish. You may have to turn this function on yourself, so consult your blogging service's help files.

- **Optimize your blog.** Make sure your blog "pings" the blog aggregators such as Technorati and Bloglines each time you've posted to your blog. That way your new content will be indexed immediately.

    An easy way to automate this is to open a free account at **www.Feedburner.com** and enable its free Pingshot feature.

More blogging fine points:

- Write in the first person. Never talk about yourself as a different being.

- Write keyword-rich headlines. Give people a reason to start reading.

- Hook your audience in the first sentence. Ask a question or pose a challenge.

- Don't get too preachy. Blog communication isn't top-down, it's a conversation.

- Focus on *you, we* and *us.*

- Don't change your blog's domain address; it's easy to lose your audience this way.

- <u>Tell the truth.</u>

- Read lots of blogs.

- Link liberally to other blogs. Your post can include an excerpt from the other blog in quotation marks, but don't include more than a paragraph or two—more than that could get you accused of copyright violation.

- Link to your previous posts.

- Don't be boring. Break some crockery. A good blog takes sides.

- Don't rant on side issues outside your blog's focus. Your audience will tire of this quickly.

- Break news.

- Be authentic.

- Tell stories. Have a conversation.

- Vary your sentence length. Frequently.

Selecting your blog publishing tool

Most bloggers don't have special blogging software installed on their PC, but work on their blog from within a Web browser. Here are the most popular blogging services:

- **Blogger.com.** Owned by Google since 2003. It's free and easy. There's an add-on program enabling you to post to your blog from Microsoft Word. You can use Blogger's free Web space, Blogspot.com, but it's best to keep your content on a domain you control, like YourName.com. Do this by using Blogger's FTP feature. For instructions: **Help.Blogger.com/bin/topic.py?topic=8917.** Other blogging systems have similar options: You can publish free on their Web space, or publish on your own domain.

- **TypePad.com.** TypePad is a flexible and professional-looking platform, but takes a bit longer to learn than Blogger. Still, you'll have many options for personalizing your blog without having to learn HTML computer code. Basic service costs $4.95 a month; the Plus level costs $8.95 a month and gives you up to three blogs hosted on your own domain. A 30-day free trial is available.

- **WordPress.com.** Set up a free blog, or upgrade to a fuller-featured service. All that's required to begin is a user name and e-mail address.

Blog-to-e-mail service

Loyal readership is key to your blog's success, so make it easy for first-time visitors to keep reading. One of the simplest ways for readers to receive your blog posts is by e-mail subscription.

FeedBlitz.com and Feedburner.com operate two popular, free blog-to-e-mail services. Both provide a snippet of code you can insert on your blog to display a sign-up box or button where readers can provide their e-mail address. Subscribers receive an e-mail digest of any new blog posts, and can click through to your site to read more.

A subscription service makes it more likely that readers will stay with you because they won't need to remember to return to your Web site. An e-mail service is a simple solution for your readers who might not understand how to use Bloglines or other newsreaders.

Only about 20 percent of blog readers understand newsreaders, "so if you're not using e-mail, you're missing 80 percent of your potential audience," says Phil Hollows, chief executive of FeedBlitz.

FeedBlitz's free service also includes some reporting tools showing how many of your e-mails are opened and which of your post headlines readers click most. Knowing which of your posts gets the biggest response is a valuable insight, showing you what content readers value most.

Some businesses who previously published monthly e-mail newsletters have abandoned their newsletters and now deliver similar content in smaller, more frequent chunks using blog-to-e-mail.

E-mail service also provides you with a valuable business asset. You'll have access to those readers directly, so you can send special messages for events like new product releases. This is why many bloggers encourage readers to sign up for e-mail delivery: It provides an automatic marketing channel for special messages about you and your products and services, without having to manually collect contact information by some other means.

The blog-to-e-mail services provide a fully automated double opt-in process, so there's no danger of your blog posts or occasional promotional messages being mistaken for spam.

Blogging systems such as Google's Blogger make it simple for you to post a Profile page, where you can enter a photograph, short biography, and additional contact information. If you think your photo will be helpful, include it on your blog. Your readers will feel a firmer connection if they can see your photo.

Blog tours

So far, we've explored techniques for luring prospects to your blog or Web site. Now we'll turn to blog outreach campaigns—going where part of your potential customer base already congregates.

You can expose your business or products to many more prospects with a series of appearances on blogs catering to your audience—a *blog tour*. Sometimes it's called *guest blogging*.

Blog tours are especially valuable for business owners unable to travel, uncomfortable with public speaking, or whose dispersed customer base makes this impractical. Blog tours can expose your business to a much large pool of prospects than by attending conferences and trade shows, while requiring less time and money. Blog tours are especially helpful in launching new products and services.

"Blogs are like rocket fuel for online publicity," said Steve O'Keefe, executive director of Patron Saint Productions, a publicity firm.

Blog tours are also a good deal for the host blogger, who gets free content for his or her readers.

Typical blog tours include these elements:

- An **guest column** displayed on the host blog to publicize the tour appearance.

- A one-day **appearance**, beginning with an opening statement, a short essay. Then the floor is open for discussion.

- **Follow-up visits** for the next four to seven days to answer questions and comments from blog readers.

Targeting host blogs

Your first step in arranging a blog tour is finding potential host blogs. Find the most popular blogs read by your target market. Some likely candidates may spring to mind, but new blogs can gain readership quickly, so it's worth surveying the field periodically.

Building your list of target blogs requires some legwork because there is no current, comprehensive directory of all blogs. To determine the popularity, authority and quality of blogs in your niche, you'll need to sample the content yourself.

Start your search here:

- **www.Technorati.com.** This site lists the top 100 most popular blogs at **Technorati.com/pop/blogs**. But to find niche content, you'll need to look beyond these mainstream blogs. Consult the advanced search tool, **Technorati.com/search**, where you can drill down into specific topics.

- **www.Blogsearch.Google.com.** Type in keywords related to your business. Ignore results from personal blogs that focus on the blog author and get little traffic.

- **www.Forbes.com/bow/b2c/main.jhtml.** Forbes' "Best of the Web" directory reviews blogs with high-quality content.

Once you've identified a list of potential blog hosts, prioritize them by three criteria: activity level, reader involvement and traffic volume.

- **Activity level.** How frequently do new posts appear on the blog? Bloggers usually must post new content a few times a week to sustain a loyal readership. Scan the past few months of blog archives to determine the posting frequency.

- **Reader involvement.** How often do readers chime in with thoughtful comments? The vast majority of blogs allow readers to follow up with their own commentary. The frequency and thoughtfulness of reader comments indicates audience engagement.

- **Traffic volume.** Traffic is the natural result of audience loyalty and involvement, and it's an objective measure of a blog's impact. A handy yardstick for measuring blog traffic is **www.Alexa.com**, which provides estimated traffic reports on many Web sites.

At Alexa.com, click Traffic Rankings at the top navigation bar. Enter the address of the blog you want to evaluate and click Get Traffic Details. For most blogs, you'll see an Alexa rank from 1 (the most-visited site on the Web) to about 5 million, meaning very low readership. For the top 100,000 sites, Alexa provides detailed traffic estimates. Under the heading **Explore this site**, you'll see these links:

- **Traffic Details** shows the blog's relative reach and number of page views, and whether traffic is trending up or down.

- **Related Links** shows other sites popular with the same audience. Here you can discover more blogs frequented by your target audience.

- **Sites Linking In** shows which sites, ranked by authority, have incoming links to the blog. Follow these links, and you'll find more sites targeting your audience.

Depending on the size and nature of your potential customer base, you may find only a few relevant quality blogs, and that's fine. It's better to focus on a small, well-qualified audience who will respond to your message instead of a general audience where you'll have little impact.

Alexa's reports aren't foolproof; they're drawn from a small sample of Web users who use its browser toolbar. Rankings for high-traffic sites are more statistically accurate than reports for niche sites. In any case, Alexa is a handy, free source of objective information about Web traffic, and is more accurate than anecdotal reports. Bloggers and Webmasters are notorious for overestimating their traffic.

Alexa, which is a subsidiary of Amazon.com, isn't limited to blogs, so you can use it to find all sorts of Web sites targeting your niche. Another good source of traffic estimates is **www.MetricsMarket.com**.

Google PageRank

Another way of determining how much juice a blog has is Google PageRank. It's a patented method Google uses to rank the importance of Web sites on a scale of one to 10 based on the authority of incoming links. Google offers a free toolbar you can use to check rankings:

http://toolbar.google.com

Quality blogs and Web sites will have a PageRank of at least five. To determine PageRank, check the blog's main page or a Web site's home page; other pages often are unranked.

Building your guest column

Now that you've identified where you'd like to appear on your blog tour, the next step is creating your guest column. The guest column is an online document providing a description of you and your business, along with one or more photographs.

Your guest column serves three purposes:

- To convince the blogger to host your appearance.

- To promote your appearance to the blog's readers.

- To prepare the blog audience to discuss your ideas and products.

Essential information like your name and business name should be embedded and visible on the photos of the cover art and author photo. That way, if a Webmaster accidentally leaves out part of your text—or it's deleted at some point—readers will still have enough information to find your Web site. If possible, combine all the elements of your guest column into a single document to ensure it's displayed properly and nothing is omitted.

A typical excerpt includes these elements:

- A brief description of your products and services, and your existing customer base.

- Features and pricing of your products and services.

- Testimonials from satisfied customers.

- Links to your Web site or to online retailers where your products are sold.

Guest columns that sell

Imagine you're riding in an elevator with a potential customer. You have 20 seconds before the elevator door opens and your companion leaves. What can you say to compel him or her to walk to the nearest retailer and buy your product as soon as the door opens? The answer is the heart of your guest column.

More elements for a compelling guest column:

- **Give chunks, not boulders.** Confine the discussion to *the most essential, engaging* nuggets of information you can provide. One way to build an effective guest column is by compiling a short list of hints, like "Top 10 ways to save money when buying a car" or "Three ways to ask someone on a date."

- **News angle.** Try to find a news hook to pique interest. Is there a current controversy or movie related to your field? Topicality is blog oxygen. For fiction and nonfiction, a strong current-events hook can persuade A-list bloggers to host your tour.

- **Benefits, not features.** What makes your product or service unique, and what can it do for the customer better than competitors? If you've received a truly impressive testimonial or endorsement, include it.

- **White space.** Break up your text. Separate paragraphs with blank lines, inserting some white space between the gray blocks of text. Readers are more likely to read your excerpt if they can scan chunks of text.

- **All together now.** If your guest column is accompanied by more than one image, assemble everything in a layout file in PDF or HTML format. This prevents the blogger or Webmaster from losing a piece of your excerpt.

Don't send your excerpt as an e-mail attachment. Most people are apprehensive of receiving files from unfamiliar people. Instead, post the document on a dedicated page on your domain, and provide the link. Then your hosts can copy the document or link to it. After you've posted the file on your domain, don't delete it, because some blogs will link to your page instead of keeping the material on their site. The excerpt on your domain may get traffic for years to come.

Your pitch to bloggers

Now your column is ready and you've compiled a list of blogs for your tour. It's time to pitch your tour to the host bloggers. Contact each blogger individually by e-mail, explaining why your appearance would be of interest. Provide two or three compelling reasons why your tour will be thought-provoking and entertaining for *this blog's audience*.

Start with your top prospects and work your way down as time permits. Contact bloggers directly; don't simply leave a comment on their blog and hope they notice it. Most blogs have a mechanism for contacting the blogger through an e-mail address or contact form.

Sometimes the more popular a blogger is, the harder it is to get their attention. If you can't find contact information, look at the bottom of the home page, where you may see instructions for contacting the "Webmaster." Sometimes an "advertise with us" link is the most reliable way of reaching a decision-maker.

Tailor your pitch for each blogger, addressing them by name, otherwise your message can be mistaken for spam. Provide your complete contact information including phone number, which also differentiates your message from spam. The subject line of your e-mail must be specific; a generic "Please read this" often is deleted unread.

The guest column includes everything the blogger needs to decide whether to approve your tour appearance. If approved, a copy of the excerpt can be posted at the host blog to promote your appearance in the days preceding the tour. Schedule no more than three to five blogs per week, which should keep you busy.

A sample pitch

Here's a sample script for pitching your blog tour:

SUBJECT: [YOUR NAME] as guest on [BLOG NAME]

Dear [BLOGGER NAME]

I'm a regular reader of your blog, and believe it's one of the best sites about [TOPIC]. I'm writing to see if you would consider having me as a guest on your blog on Monday, May 9, to discuss [TOPIC].

I believe my [PRODUCTS, SERVICES] are of particular interest to your readership. [REASONS, BRIEFLY]

I'm hoping to have a dialog with your readers. If you approve, I'll take a day on your blog, make an opening statement, and respond to comments as long as they keep coming.

I hope you'll give this a try. I've prepared a guest column in an HTML document, which you can view here at my site: http://www.example.com. You're free to reproduce this document on your site or provide links.

Thanks for your consideration,
[SIGNATURE]
[PHYSICAL ADDRESS]
[PHONE NUMBER]

Not every blogger will accept your pitch, and you shouldn't take the rejections personally—an acceptance rate of 25 percent is a good target. Some sites simply don't use content that isn't written by its staff. Often blogs run by newspapers or magazines don't use third-party content except in sections labeled "opinion" or "to the editor."

As realistically as possible, pitch yourself as a potential long-term partner, not a drive-by opportunist. Successful blog tours will prompt return invitations and can launch a mutually beneficial relationship.

Your guest appearance

On the day of your blog tour appearance, open with a short statement, recapping the themes expressed in your guest column, and ask the blog audience for its reaction. Depending on how the blogger administers the site, you may be given a login and password for the site, or simply e-mail your material to the blogger.

Reaction from the blog audience can continue for several days, giving you the opportunity to reappear, replying to comments and answering questions.

Blog conversation

When responding to a blog audience, be succinct and keep the conversation moving. Blog conversation is a two-way street, and exchanging ideas makes compelling content. At the end of each of your responses, conclude with a question, such as "What's your take on that?" or "How do you feel about this?"

Be prepared for the occasional rude or embarrassing question. For example, if your topic is barbecuing, be ready for questions from animal-rights activists. Feel free to ignore off-topic comments, and simply continue with your message, but don't shy away from substantive arguments.

At each stop on your blog tour, mention your previous appearances on other blogs and provide the links. This will generate continued readership and cross-linking among blogs.

Encore appearances

Blog tours don't always cause a big spike in sales or new clients, but they do contribute to word of mouth. Each time you appear in front of your target audience, it's a plus. When a blog appearance goes particularly well, don't let it end there. Offer to write a monthly guest column for the blog in exchange for a link to your site.

Multimedia

As high-speed Internet service becomes more common, audio and video content are becoming valuable publicity tools. Multimedia is particularly effective for niche businesses and newcomers who haven't attracted much market share.

Multimedia grabs the attention of younger people who spend more leisure time online, while consuming less traditional media like newspapers and television. Meanwhile, production and distribution of trailers is getting easier and cheaper by the day, thanks to inexpensive video cameras and free hosting sites like **www.YouTube.com**.

Online *trailers*, an increasingly popular tool, often resemble movie previews, music videos or talk shows. Even though trailers are promotional materials, the people who choose to watch often perceive them as interesting, valuable content. Any sort of product or service that you can talk about or represent visually can be presented in a trailer.

Trailers are an effective tool for products that can't afford traditional advertising or whose disparate market makes them hard to target. Consider a trailer as something akin to a TV infomercial, a message that appears on a cable network of 5 million channels—except you have global reach and very low costs. The videos can contain a "buy it now" link or a link to more information.

Successful trailers are an example of *viral marketing* because of the huge exposure gained through Web links and e-mails. Thanks largely to e-mail forwarding, a trailer for the humor book *Yiddish with Dick and Jane* was seen by 1 million people during its first week, helping to sell 150,000 copies of the book. You can view the video at:

www.VidLit.com/yidlit

Here are more examples of successful promotions employing online video:

• Chipotle sponsored a contest challenging college students to make a 30-second commercial about the restaurant chain and upload it to YouTube. A $10,000 prize was offered for the video viewed most often. The top effort, by students from Nebraska, garnered 8 million views, and the second-place video had 7.7 million views. In all, the contest resulted in 17.3 million views from a promotion budget of just $50,000. Chipotle estimates that buying the same amount of exposure through online advertising would have cost $346,000, and the equivalent in television ads would have cost $434,000.

• The Wendy's hamburger chain has placed humorous videos created by its ad agency on YouTube and gotten hundreds of thousands of people to view them. More than 600,000 viewers watched its "Molly Grows Up" spoof of a puberty education film, and thousands more watched its "Frosty vs. Fries" and "Space Chili Cheeseburger Deluxe" spots.

• Domino's Pizza created fictionalized viral videos to promote a special offer of large pizzas for $9.99. The "Anything Goes Deal" videos featured "larger than life" characters offering to sell expensive items. One video showed a spoiled young girl who received an expensive sports car for her birthday but didn't like the color, so she sold it on eBay for $9.99. The videos were viewed by thousands on MySpace and other social networking sites, and generated coverage in newspapers and blogs.

Marketing with viral videos

You can spend practically as much or as little as you'd like producing a trailer. Do-it-yourself videos are a realistic option, thanks to falling prices of digital camcorders.

If you have a PC with Windows XP, you can edit digital video yourself using a free program in your Accessories folder called "Movie Maker." If you're a Mac user, there's iMovie.

Author Chris Epting scored big using YouTube to promote his 2007 book *Led Zeppelin Crashed Here*, a guide to "rock and roll landmarks." Six months before publication, Epting began posting a series of trailers, featuring photos he shot for the book and classic-rock soundtracks. The videos prompted thousands of rock fans to write to Epting with suggestions for the book and requests to buy it.

Start with a video that shows some of your customers and the products and services you offer. Keep the length under a few minutes if possible.

When uploading your video to YouTube or other sites, add tags that describe what the video shows. Don't skimp on the tags because that's how most people will find your video. And don't forget to show the URL to your Web site at the video's beginning and end.

Podcasting for publicity

A podcast is an audio file hosted on the Web, available to listeners anytime. Audio recordings you may already have—such as interviews or speeches—can be repurposed as a podcast, providing Internet users with yet another way to discover you and your business.

Some podcasts are a recurring feature, sometimes called a podiobook. Perhaps you'll decide to provide your audio content for free to help generate word of mouth for your business. Some create value-added podcasts and charge subscription fees, making them a virtual extension of their business.

Users can listen to your podcasts on their PCs, or download them to a portable music player such as an iPod. The word *podcast* is a combination of the word iPod and broadcasting, but no iPod is required—anyone with speakers on their computer can listen.

Just like blog-reading provides insights for building your own blog, listening to podcasts will inspire ideas for producing your own audio content. Here are some directories where you can sample what's available:

- **iTunes:** www.Apple.com/itunes/podcasts. Here you can sample or subscribe to podcasts.

- **Yahoo Podcasts:** Podcasts.yahoo.com. Listen to podcasts using your Web browser, or download files.

- **PodioCast:** PodioCast.com. Serialized audiobooks.

- **LibriVox:** Librivox.org. Free audiobooks from the public domain.

Podcasts can be used to take advantage of sudden opportunities. For example, in 2007 author Mignon Fogarty, host of the Grammar Girl podcast, was unexpectedly booked to appear on *Oprah*. In response, she produced an audio file of a book she was in the process of writing, and uploaded it to Audible.com just before her TV appearance. The hour-long $4.95 audio went to No. 1 on iTunes, and she cashed in on the publicity even though the book wasn't finished.

To record material for your podcasts, all that's required is a microphone and PC. Free software for recording and editing podcasts is offered at **www.Audacity.Sourceforge.net**. Another option is **www.HipCast.com**, which lets you create podcasts through your Web browser or telephone, then post it to your blog or Web site. For Mac users, GarageBand is a good podcast tool.

Here's a guide for making your own podcasts:

www.How-To-Podcast-Tutorial.com

Tag – You're it!

Tagging is a relatively new but increasingly popular way for Internet users to organize things by using personal keywords. Tags can be used to label all kinds of items found on the Web, including books, product reviews, pictures and videos. Already, some are calling tags "the Internet's Dewey Decimal System."

Users create tags for their own purposes, but they can be used by anyone. With enough people participating, tags can become an effortless, super-accurate recommendations system among like-minded people. The site that popularized tagging was **www.Flickr.com**, a social site where users store, organize and share their digital photos. Instead of using a single category for organizing pictures— like a folder labeled "2005 Vacation"—members use one- or two-word tags like waterfall, solar eclipse, Houston, Joe or 2005. This way, photos can be grouped and discovered in multiple ways.

Tags are a form of *metadata*, which means, literally, "data about data." Tagging creates a *folksonomy*, a bottom-up method of categorization. *Taxonomies* are governed by experts like librarians and botanists who want to show hierarchical relationships. Folksonomies are built by amateurs but can be more helpful for users.

Folksonomies are gaining steam, aided by the easy exchange of ideas online. Often taxonomies aren't specific, flexible or current enough. Increasingly, people use tags to tap collective wisdom.

Amazon tags

Why should you care about tags? Because tags are an important new way for readers to discover you or your merchandise. Tagging is an individual activity with global utility. Each product listed for sale on Amazon.com, for example, can be assigned its own unique "category" yet reside in thousands of other categories at the same time.

Amazon added its tagging feature in 2005, and made it more prominent—higher on product detail pages—than its traditional category lists. Amazon tags are publicly viewable unless users designate them as private. You can manage your tags through a **Your Tags** field at the bottom of every Amazon page.

If you have a product sold on Amazon, you can increase its visibility by adding the obvious keywords appropriate to that product. For example, one of the digital cameras for sale on Amazon has 60 tags, including:

- Canon
- image stabilization
- powershot
- compact
- cam for Mary
- wide-angle

Amazon tags are indexed by Google and other search engines.

As users of Amazon and other retailing sites begin to use tagging, finding niche products will become easier than ever. Tags assigned to obscure products will be rare but instantly apparent. A few common tags will be used by huge numbers of users and visible to everyone: The five most-used tags on Amazon are DVD, music, books, fantasy and anime. Most tags, including the more useful ones, will be seldom used, such as *bizarre apocalpytacism,* Amazon's least-used tag. Many tags will be used by just a few people, perhaps assigned to only one product, enabling a niche of one.

As a consumer, here are some ways you might use tags on Amazon:

- **To organize your books.** Tag the books you already own and organize them as you wish. If you don't agree with the category groups as Amazon has arranged them, make up your own. Tag the items that matter to you with categories you care about.

- **To remember merchandise you're considering buying.** If one of your tagged items is intended for a Christmas gift, you can tag the book "Xmas" or "present"— tags that aren't very useful to others. Tags like "real best picture of 2004" are better.

- **Personalized recommendations based on tags.** Go to www.Amazon.com/yourstore and click on tags shown under the heading "Recommendations Based on Your Tags."

You can view all your tags on Amazon here:

www.Amazon.com/gp/tagging/manage-tags

Here you can add or delete tags, and designate them public or private. You can also edit or remove tags you've created by clicking on <u>Edit</u> from the product's Amazon page.

You can view the tags for any Amazon customer who's made at least one purchase, unless they've chosen to keep their tags private.

Tag-based marketing

As a marketer, you should use tags to stay current on how people are finding and sharing information in your field. For example, you can subscribe to RSS feeds to monitor how consumers tag information related to your area of business. For example, to keep tabs on organic fruit, you could bookmark this page:

http://del.icio.us/tag/organic+fruit

By bookmarking this page, you'll get updates on interesting links consumers are discovering and sharing about "organic fruit." You'll have a global focus group working for you 24 hours a day, seven days a week.

Or let's imagine you want to monitor all the books to which Amazon users assign the tag "murder mystery." You can watch:

www.Amazon.com/
gp/tagging/glance/murder+mystery

Should you tag your own products? Certainly, but anyone using tags for marketing should be transparent about it, says Steve Rubel, author of the blog Micro Persuasion. In other words, if you're plugging your own products, don't pretend you're an uninterested bystander. Don't hide your identity, and don't spam.

Problems with tags

One weakness of tags is that the same tag can mean two completely different things to different people. For example, a recent memoir by CNN correspondent Anderson Cooper is tagged by various Amazon users with "news memoir," "blue eyes," and "hunk." Since "hunk" is a tag with many possible meanings, it appears on many products with seemingly no connection—like a movie starring Russell Crowe, the DVD *Forrest Gump*, heavy sweaters, and books about the "chunky" clothing style.

Conversely, various people will assign different tags to the same thing—one person may tag photos of their dog "cocker spaniel" while another user tags the same photo "canines." A search for the tag "dogs" might not turn up either photo. With books, an Amazon user may assign the tag "Christmas" to a book about baseball, meaning that she intends to buy it as a Christmas gift. Meanwhile, customers using the tag "Christmas" to search for Christmas books will be frustrated.

Like any valuable tool, tags can be abused, too. If tagging goes mainstream, spammers will try exploiting tags by adding their irrelevant tags to popular items.

Tags aren't necessarily linked with semantics. So the word "blow" could be used as a tag for wind, cocaine, sucking, breath, or a picture of a tornado, or the sound of air rushing. The user of the tag, not a search engine, decides how the meaning fits for them.

Advocates of tagging assert these fears are overblown. With enough users, tags become self-correcting, so inappropriate or useless tags will be drowned out by the good ones.

The social jungle

The conventional wisdom is that Web. 2.0 and social networking emerged in 2004. But it really was launched during the mid-1990s by Amazon.com. Amazon has all the features of most social-networking sites such as MySpace, and then some. If your product is sold on the site—or if there are related books or other products sold there—Amazon can be a valuable platform.

Amazon friends

"Amazon friends" resembles the friendship feature on MySpace and other networking sites, and is gaining prominence as Amazon increasingly emphasizes its "community" aspects. Designating someone your Amazon friend provides an easy way for you to track his or her community participation on Amazon. Depending on the privacy settings on both profiles, you can view each other's recent purchases, Wish Lists, upcoming birthdays, and e-mail address.

Adding someone as an Amazon friend can help you find people interested in networking or reviewing your product. To make an Amazon friend invitation, scroll about two-thirds of the way down your profile page, **www.Amazon.com/gp/pdp**. You'll see a heading for **Amazon Friends & Interesting People** and a search box where you can input names or e-mail addresses.

Clicking on the person's name or e-mail address allows you to send a message that will be forwarded by Amazon.

Amazon users have three options in responding to a friend invitation:

• **Accept** — Both members become each other's Amazon friend and appear on each other's list of Friends.

• **Decline** — The sender's invitation is removed from a list of pending invitations on the invitee's profile. The sender isn't notified the invitation is declined, and is free to send future invitations.

• **Decline and block** — Declines the invitation and prevents future Friends invitations. The sender's name appears in a "Blocked People" list visible to you on your profile, and you have the option of unblocking them later.

• **Ignore** — The default option, and probably the most popular. The recipient ignores the Friends invitation and deletes the e-mail.

Amazon users have the option of receiving friend invitations only from people who know their e-mail address and enter it correctly into the invitation form. Here's how to manage this setting:

1. On your profile page, scroll down the middle column to the section labeled **Amazon Friends & Interesting People**.

2. Click <u>See your pending invitations</u>.

3. At the bottom, in the section labeled **Blocking Preference**, check the box **Block invitations from people who don't know my e-mail address** and click the yellow button **Save preferences**.

Interesting people

Amazon's Interesting People feature lets you book-mark users to easily view their latest Amazon activity—customer reviews, tagging activity, etc. To add someone to your interesting people list, go to their profile page and, in the box labeled **Your Actions**, click the link <u>Add to Interesting People</u>. You can search for people to add to your list by selecting **People** from the search pull-down menu at the top left corner of your profile page.

Listmania

Listmania lists allow any Amazon user—customers, authors, music lovers, movie buffs—to create lists of their favorite items organized by theme. Listmanias appear in various places on Amazon, like product detail pages and alongside search results. Listmanias that mention your product can expose it to thousands of potential customers on Amazon, and the list can even appear in Google search results for associated keywords.

Listmanias are ranked by popularity among shoppers, based on viewership and the number of votes calling it "helpful." For example, one popular list is dedicated to novelist Nick Hornby, and was compiled by one of his fans. Under each novel is a pithy quote from the Listmania author, just enough to convey the gist of each book and why it appears. The list includes most of Hornby's books, other books Hornby edited or wrote introductions for, and a few other novels by writers with similar styles. See this list at:

www.Amazon.com/gp/richpub/listmania/
fullview/1X1GGDBXARHZ6

See the 100 most popular Listmanias here:

www.Amazon.com/
gp/richpub/listmania/toplists

Niche products stand to gain the most from Listmanias. The more focused a Listmania is, the more helpful it is to buyers hungry for specific information—so the more likely it is to be noticed, read carefully, and acted on. Niche Listmanias have less competition—Amazon can show only so many "Harry Potter" Listmanias while the thousands of similar lists wait in a queue. But your Listmania about "Organic Strawberries" may pop up in front of every single customer looking for a relevant products.

To write a Listmania, click on the link at the bottom of your Amazon profile page, "More to Explore." Or start your list by clicking on the link Create Your Own List on an existing Listmania. Then:

1. Go to your Amazon Profile at: **www.Amazon.com/gp/pdp**.
2. Near the bottom of the middle column, in the section **More to Explore**, click Listmania Lists.
3. Click Create your first one now or Create another list.
4. Enter a title for your list and enter your "qualifications" such as "business owner" or "consultant." For your title, think of a blurb that will catch the eye of anyone shopping for a related item.
5. Enter products sold on Amazon, including your own, and write a short comment for each.
6. Click the **Preview** button and check for typos.

7. Edit your list, and when satisfied, click the button **Publish list**. You can edit it later if you wish.

Your Listmania lists will appear on your Amazon Profile and in search results related to items on your list. From your Profile, you'll have the option of editing your lists or deleting them.

So You'd Like to . . . guides

Have you ever wished you could submit a how-to essay to your local newspaper that demonstrates your expertise and helps publicize your business? You can accomplish much the same feat on Amazon by writing a *So You'd Like to ...* guide, which could be read by more people than a newspaper article.

Amazon's *So You'd Like to ...* guides somewhat resemble Listmania, but are more like tutorials. They're time-consuming and require considerably more original writing than Listmanias, but are consulted often, especially in niche topics. Some rewritten content from your blog or Web site might serve as the basis of a guide.

For example, you could write a guide called "Beginner's Guide to Growing Organic Fruit." In the course of writing your guide, you can link to items from Amazon's garden section, general gardening reference books, and your title *Organic Strawberries*.

To include products in your guide you'll need to look up their 10-digit ASIN (Amazon Standard Identification Number) that appears on the item's detail page under the heading **Product Details**.

To get started writing a guide, go to your Amazon profile at **www.Amazon.com/gp/pdp**. Near the bottom of the middle column, in the section labeled **More to Explore**, click on <u>So You'd Like to ... Guides</u>, then click on <u>Create a guide</u>. Guides must include at least three products sold on Amazon and may have a maximum of 50. The first three mentioned in your guide will become featured items that appear at the top of your guide when it appears on Amazon's site.

Break up your guide into sections every few paragraphs by inserting a subheading like this:

<HEADLINE: (Type your headline here)>

Before finishing, copy your text into a word processor and spell-check it. After you're finished writing and editing your guide, click on the **Publish** button.

Later you can add more products or content to your guides by editing them. From your Profile at **www.Amazon.com/gp/pdp**, click <u>So You'd Like to ... Guides</u> near the bottom of the middle column, then click the **Edit** button on the right of the guide you wish to change.

Writing product reviews

No matter what type of business you're in, you can build your reputation by writing Amazon reviews of related books and products. Writing a compelling review exposes thousands of Amazon shoppers to the names of you and your business.

If your product is sold on Amazon, you can insert a link to its product page in your review. Keep in mind that this might be seen as self-serving by some. In any case, don't hide your identity or cover up any financial interest you may have with the products you're discussing.

Many Amazon reviewers add a plug for their product or business within their Amazon pen name, which is displayed with the reviews, such as Thomas Edison, inventor of the light bulb.'

To change the way your name is displayed, visit your Amazon Profile at **www.Amazon.com/gp/pdp**. In the left column, in the **About Me** section, click change name.

To write an Amazon product review, go to the product's detail page and scroll down to the section labeled **Spotlight Reviews**, then click the link Write an online review. The maximum length of reviews is 1,000 words, and the recommended length is 75 to 300 words. The title of your review is limited to 60 characters.

Amazon strongly discourages the following elements in customer reviews:

• Dates of promotional tours or lectures that become outdated.

• Commenting on previous reviews (other reviews might be edited or deleted in the future).

• Profanity or cruel remarks.

• Single-word reviews.

• Contact information such as phone numbers, addresses or URLs.

• Discussing the item's price, availability, or shipping information.

• Asking people to "vote" for your review.

Check your review for spelling and typos by running the text through a word processor. Break up your text with a blank line between each paragraph to add white space. Often reviews show up immediately on the product's detail page, but sometimes it takes several days. To ask about the status of a review, write to **community-help@amazon.com**.

The more helpful your review is to Amazon users, the more often it will be voted "helpful" and have an impact. Spotlight Reviews have the most impact since they appear first. Your review has a better chance of becoming a Spotlight if it's submitted soon after the product's introduction, and after a few other reviews have already appeared.

Amapedia

Amazon launched Amapedia (originally called ProductWikis) in April 2006, allowing customers to write their own articles, or wikis, on any product page. The Amazon wikis resemble user-generated content popularized by Wikipedia.org, a free online encyclopedia.

The concept behind wikis is that anyone can write one, and that anyone else can come along later and correct mistakes. It's unclear how useful wikis will be for Amazon shoppers—will shoppers want to read miscellaneous writings by other shoppers, or care enough to correct mistakes?

Wikis are supposed to differ from product reviews and other user-generated content in one important way: Writers are supposed to stick to facts, and avoid injecting their opinions.

What could hurt the utility of wikis is their misuse by spammers. And there's nothing to prevent competitors from adding false information. Wikis are supposed to be self-correcting, but experience shows this doesn't always happen.

Customer Discussions

Customer Discussions are a relatively new feature on Amazon allowing customers to ask questions, share insights, and give opinions about products. However, since this feature appears near the bottom of increasingly crowded Amazon detail pages, customer discussions tend to be used infrequently, except on the pages of very popular products. No mechanism exists to notify product suppliers of questions requiring a follow-up.

Getting recommended

Good sales are a self-fulfilling prophecy on Amazon. The more people who buy your product, the easier it becomes for the next shopper to discover it. When Amazon notices your product is selling, it automatically displays it higher in its search results and higher in its category lists. And most importantly, Amazon starts plugging your product into automated recommendations on its Web site and in e-mails to customers.

Recommendations are Amazon's biggest sales engine, after keyword searches. Sixty-six percent of sales are to returning customers, many of them acting on automated recommendations for items popular with customers with similar buying histories.

Because they are personalized, Amazon's recommendations are network-powered word of mouth—more effective than a highway billboard seen by everyone in town. And as long as your product keeps selling, Amazon continues recommending it month after month, year after year, to its likely buyers.

Personalized stores

Each of Amazon's 65 million customers sees a unique store. The layout is personalized, based on which items the customer previously viewed or purchased. Each customer has a recommendations list, based on which products are bought most frequently by other customers with similar buying histories.

If you have an Amazon account, view your recommendations here:

www.Amazon.com/yourstore

Buyers see product recommendations in several places:

• On Amazon's home page, where it says, **Hello, [NAME], we have recommendations for you.** Click here to view all your recommendations.

• In e-mails titled **Amazon.com Recommends** ... and **New for You**, periodically sent to Amazon customers.

• In the **Gold Box** treasure chest icon at the top right of Amazon's home page. Clicking the box reveals special offers on merchandise on your recommended list.

- In a product's **Also-Bought** list. Most product detail pages on Amazon includes a list with the headline **Customers who bought this item also bought**. The Also-Bought list shows the five other items bought most frequently by customers who also purchased the displayed product.

- An extended Also-Bought list that includes many more titles is accessible from each product's detail page at the link <u>Explore similar items</u>. Buyers can view the same list during the checkout process by viewing **Customers who bought [Item] also bought...**

The wisdom of crowds

Amazon's recommendations aren't just a computer talking, it's the collective judgment of millions of people acting independently in their own self-interest. Amazon is an effective word-of-mouth generator because it measures not what people *say*, but what they *do*. People don't always recommend favorite products to each of their friends and acquaintances. But Amazon factors each buying decision into its recommendations for like-minded customers.

Just as a well-programmed computer can defeat a master chess player, automated recommendations can suggest just the right item, including things that would never occur to a clerk in a store, says Amazon chief executive Jeff Bezos:

 I remember one of the first times this struck me. The main book on the page was about Zen. There were other suggestions for Zen books, but in the middle of those was a [recommended] book on "How to have a clutter-free desk."

That's not something that a human editor would ever pick. But statistically, the people who were interested in the Zen books also wanted clutter-free desks. The computer is blind to the fact that these things are dissimilar in some way to humans. It looks right through that and says, "Yes, try this." And it works.

Fine-tuning recommendations

Because so many sales can result from Amazon recommendations, it's worth spending a few minutes looking under the hood. Here's a shortcut to your Amazon recommendations:

www.Amazon.com/yourstore

On the left, click <u>Books</u> or any other category to filter out other types of merchandise. Now, directly below each of the recommended items, you'll see the reason it's being recommended, such as: **Recommended because you purchased [Item].**

For each recommended item, you can refine the system by indicating:

- Whether you own the item.

- Whether you're just "not interested" in the recommended item.

- Your rating for the item on a scale of 1 to 5, with 5 meaning "I love it."

Few Amazon customers take the time to confirm this raw data in Amazon's recommendations engine, and as a result it can spit out some wacky suggestions. For example, if you've purchased gifts for children or friends that you wouldn't buy for yourself, the result is often faulty recommendations.

In some cases, Amazon will guess correctly which of your purchases are gifts—for example, when you ship an item to a different address—and excludes them from recommendations. If not, here's how to exclude inappropriate products from your recommendations:

• Near the top of your recommendations list is the text, "These recommendations are based on items you own and more."

• Clicking you own shows the list of products Amazon knows you've purchased.

• To exclude certain products from the recommendations system, uncheck the box labeled **Use to make recommendations**.

You can also improve your recommendations by letting Amazon know about items you've purchased elsewhere.

The star ratings you assign to products on this list won't be visible to other Amazon users, but the ratings can affect which items get recommended to whom and how often.

Social media, social search

In the mid 1990s, Yahoo, the first popular Web portal, guided most Internet traffic with a simple hand-picked menu of sites. Yahoo's editors decided which Web sites were worth pointing to, and that's where the traffic went. At the time, it seemed like a good system, and much more efficient than search engines, which tended to spit out mountains of irrelevant results. Back then, it sometimes seemed easier to find a needle in a haystack than to find anything with a search engine.

Then Google built a better mousetrap. Instead of relying on humans to figure out which content is best, Google's computers determined relevance and authority. Google's PageRank system considers not only the words contained on a Web page, but also how many related sites link in. Each incoming link is a vote on a page's importance, helping it rise to the top of Google's search results.

As good as Google's system is, however, it can't always deliver relevant results, particularly for specialized content. Sometimes providing good search results requires direct human brainpower, something provided by *social search* tools. Social search works best in deep niches, where people who truly understand the content render judgments. In these cases, social search can be more accurate than Google's algorithmic search, which counts links only.

Why should you care about social search? Because more and more people are using it to find the exact product or service they want.

Here's what can happen if your company's Web site or blog is mentioned favorably on a social search service—a flood of 5,000 to 10,000 visitors can come to your site within hours. This crowd can include thousands of folks highly passionate about your topic, and those nearly impossible to reach through traditional advertising or publicity.

Dozens of popular sites have emerged in the past few years providing tools for search, social networking, and social bookmarking:

del.icio.us

http://del.icio.us was launched in 2004 and is a dominant social bookmarking site. It's a handy way for people to store their favorite Web bookmarks online where they're portable, instead of on the PC, confined to one machine.

For example, a student writing a dissertation might use del.icio.us to track all their source materials and commentary. Instead of having a hard-to-read list of bookmarks in a drop-down menu on their Web browser, users just consult their del.icio.us page to view their favorite Web resources, along with their own annotations.

To organize their bookmarks, del.icio.us users tag them with personalized keywords, like a folksonomy, instead of using a hierarchical taxonomy or set categories.

This makes it easier for del.icio.us users to find relevant resources intuitively.

But here's the ultimate value of social bookmarking: the ability to share bookmarks with others, instantly tapping into collective wisdom. For example, let's imagine you want to learn about tropical fish. From the del.icio.us home page, you search for "tropical fish." Instead of finding only the most *universally popular* sites Google shows you, on del.icio.us you find the *favorite* resources of tropical-fish fanatics. These are the resources valued by the people with experience, the people who eat, breathe and sleep tropical fish.

Shared resources are the ones with real word of mouth, not just a certain number of links or brute-force advertising. The results are the best in the judgment of those who know the most. There's no substitute for recommendations by people who've consumed the content and found it important, useful or entertaining.

Search is what you do when you know what you're looking for. *Discovery* is how you find what you didn't know existed.

Smart crowds

When del.icio.us users save a Web page as a bookmark, they're "voting" for the page, much as Google's PageRank measures how popular a page is by counting incoming links. But with social bookmarks, individuals vote. With social sites, everyone votes, not just Webmasters and bloggers. Since individual Internet users vastly outnumber Webmasters or bloggers, the collective wisdom is much richer.

Once someone mentions you on del.icio.us—by book-marking your blog or Web site—it's much easier for people to find you, and you'll get a new stream of people coming to your site who are already interested in what you have to say.

You can hope that people will take it on themselves to bookmark you on del.icio.us, or you can make it easy for them. You can configure your blog to automatically insert a small **add to del.icio.us** button to the bottom of all your posts. Every reader who clicks the button casts another vote for you. For instructions on adding these buttons, see:

www.publisher.yahoo.com/social_media_tools

Vertical search

Another example of a social search tool is a *Swicki*, which improves and personalizes its results based on feedback from your site's users.

For example, imagine you publish a blog about labor unions. Your visitors frequently perform keyword searches using the word "labor" to find what they're looking for. A universal search for "labor" would produce many unhelpful results—content about pregnancy, birthing, premature births, and maternity leave.

By installing a Swicki on your site, users can customize their search results. They can vote up the relevant results they see—those on labor unions—and vote down the irrelevant results. The search engine learns from its users.

Swicki is a play on the words search and wiki, implying that its value comes from user input. The tool is provided free by a company called Eurekster. It can also produce some additional income for your site, if you elect to show the paid ads Swickis offers. For more information, see:

www.Swicki.com

You'll be able to design the look of your Swicki and receive a snippet of code to insert the Swicki into your site—the entire process takes about 20 minutes.

Another popular vertical search tool is provided by Rollyo, which promises to help users "roll your own" search engine. For details, visit:

www.Rollyo.com

Google is getting into the personalized-search field, too. In 2006 it began testing Google Customized Search, which is linked to its AdSense program. You can specify the Web sites you want searched and integrate its search box and results into your own site. See:

www.Google.com/coop/cse

Amazon Search Suggestions

Search Suggestions is a feature launched in 2006 enabling anyone with an Amazon account to add a bit of human intelligence to the site's search engine. On each product detail page, the link Make a Search Suggestion allows users to recommend tying a product to specific keywords. Users also explain why the keywords are relevant and will help people find the item.

Let's imagine your company makes custom-built stands for televisions. You could suggest the term "HDTV" for your products. That way, Amazon shoppers searching for high-definition TVs could also discover your products.

You can take advantage of Search Suggestions by linking your product with relevant words and expressions that don't appear in the title. For example, let's imagine you sell a book about predicting hurricanes. A year after your book goes on the market, the most damaging hurricane in history, a storm named Zelda, devastates the Florida coast. By entering the Search Suggestion "Hurricane Zelda," more buyers would find your book, even though it didn't contain "Zelda."

Once your Search Suggestion is approved, when customers search using your keywords, the product appears in search results along with your relevancy **explanation.**

Digg

www.Digg.com is a news community run by amateur news buffs instead of professional news editors. Members submit items of note they've found somewhere on the Web and vote for the ones they like. A typical entry might read: "A Windmill for Your Backyard? A new, affordable wind turbine promises to help homeowners fight rising energy costs." Readers would click through to the site or blog, read the original article, then vote it up (digg it) or down (undigg).

If your blog or Web site gets voted up on Digg, you can expect a crush of visitors within minutes.

Originally Digg was narrowly focused on technology news, but in 2006 it expanded into world news, entertainment, politics, and other topics. Members pride

Plug Your Business! | 113

themselves on unearthing noteworthy items that might be overlooked by traditional news sources.

Items are assigned to a category such as technology, business, gaming, or entertainment. If a story receives enough votes, it's promoted to the site's home page, where it's often read by hundreds of thousands of members who often click through to the blog or Web site for further information, or perhaps blog about it themselves.

Netscape

America Online/Netscape launched a Digg-style, user-driven news site in 2006 at **www.netscape.com**.

Flickr

www.Flickr.com is a social bookmarking site focusing solely on photographs. Amateur and professional photographers upload their favorite photos to share with friends and strangers, who can assign tags and add comments. Yahoo bought Flickr in 2005.

Popurls

www.Popurls.com is like a "greatest hits" of about 15 of the most highly trafficked social bookmarking sites, updated frequently.

Listible

www.Listible.com is a site featuring lists of users' favorite Web sites resources classified by tags such as "design," "movie," "opensource," or "firefox." Lists are popular with many Web users. Users can rate the items on the list and post comments.

Syndicating your content

Most people don't purchase a product the first time they hear of it. It can take six or seven exposures to prompt a consumer to buy. The more frequently you can pop up in front of your potential audience—providing valuable, free content—the larger your audience becomes. When Internet searchers discover valuable content, they become prime candidates for buying an item or ordering a service from someone regarded as an expert.

The benefits of posting free sample content online grow by the day. Not only can consumers find you, but reporters and news producers increasingly turn to the Internet to find expert sources and story ideas. This can lead to exposure and credibility that can't be bought at any price.

Here are some good ways of providing sample content to burnish your reputation and achieve expert status:

- **Post question-and-answer content.** On your blog or Web site, summarize the best questions you receive from readers via e-mail, phone calls, letters or personal conversations. Publish them in a question-and-answer format. This provides interesting, valuable and easy-to-read content. Q&A content is simple to produce, especially if you're already producing the raw material by answering e-mails. When you post this content publicly, your entire audience benefits, instead of just one person (although you should omit personally identifying information where appropriate). Further, Q&As expand your audience because the format boosts your visibility with search engines. Many people searching the Web actually type questions into Google, such as "How to stop thumb-sucking." You can rewrite the questions for clarity, or even write the question yourself to help illustrate a point. You can use this same type of content to build an FAQ, or Frequently Asked Questions, page on your site.

• **Participate in online discussions.** Answering queries about your topic on discussion boards and e-mail lists can lure more visitors to your site. Find relevant groups on Web boards and in groups sponsored by Yahoo, MSN, LiveJournal and America Online. Add a three- or four-line signature to the bottom of your posts, including your company name, flagship product, and Web address. Be sure to provide helpful information; don't post purely promotional messages. Follow the rules of the group, which sometimes preclude commercial content.

• **Post comments on blogs related to your topic.** Most blogs allow you to include a link back to your site in your comment. Invest the time in providing useful, thoughtful commentary, and you'll bring some new visitors to your site.

Article banks

An increasingly popular way to get exposure is by contributing to online article banks. One of the most popular,

EzineArticles.com, has more than 55,000 members who post content. Contributors aren't paid, but they figure the added exposure is worth the effort.

If your articles are accepted, they're featured on EzineArticles.com and made available for reuse on other Web sites, blogs and e-mail newsletters. Each article includes a "resource box" with links back to your site.

Although article syndication can provide great exposure, be selective about the content you contribute. Don't offer any content that appears on your site without first rewriting it. Search engines such as Google constantly filter out "duplicate content" from search results. If an article from your site appears elsewhere on the Internet, one of the Web pages probably will be deleted from search results, and chances are it will be yours. Search-engine experts call this the *duplicate content penalty*.

How duplicate content backfires

Let's imagine you operate a pottery studio, and to help promote it, you publish a pottery blog. Last year on your blog, you wrote a nifty tutorial on fixing broken pottery. Word has gotten around, and now every pottery site on the Internet links to your pottery-repair page. Because of all these links, your page is the top Google result for "repairing pottery," "fixing pottery," and several related queries. That single page is your Web site's crown jewel, accounting for half your new visitors and a good portion of your business.

Now let's imagine you try to squeeze even *more* traffic from your pottery-repair article. You post it to EzineArticles.com, without changing much except to add the links back to your site. Meanwhile, you upload the same article to other syndication sites like GoArticles.com and Idea-Marketers.com.

Now you sit back and wait for the extra traffic, but the exact opposite happens—you see less traffic, not more. Now that your article appears on a bigger, more popular site, it's likely that Google will send searchers there instead of sending them to your site. Google has made a quick calculation of which site is more authoritative, and because EzineArticles.com has more links than your site, it wins. Google doesn't care that you wrote the article and have the Internet's best pottery site.

The lesson is, keep your most valuable content on your site exclusively. And if you're going to syndicate existing content, rewrite it substantially so the search engines don't penalize you for it.

Google's Adam Lasnik, the company's "search evangelist," offers two tips for avoiding the duplicate content penalty:

• If you syndicate an article containing the same or very similar language that appears somewhere on your site, ensure the syndicated article includes a link back to the original article on your site. Don't include only a link to your home page or some other page.

• Minimize boilerplate language on all your content. For example, instead of including lengthy copyright notices at the bottom of all your Web pages, include a brief summary with a link to a page containing your full copyright notice.

None of these safeguards, however, is foolproof. The only sure way to avoid the duplicate content penalty is by syndicating original material only, and keeping your best material exclusive to your site.

Really Simple Syndication

RSS, or Really Simple Syndication, is a Web feed that allows people to view summaries of your blog posts. Readers are automatically notified when you post new material. Most blogging software automatically publishes an RSS feed for you, or you can open a free account with Feedburner, which will publish an RSS feed for you with several enhancements:

www.Feedburner.com

Although an RSS feed makes your blog more visible, there are also a few disadvantages. For example, readers who can view all your blog content within an RSS reader may quit visiting your Web site, and won't be exposed to other types of content. You can minimize this problem by syndicating a brief summary of your blog posts, perhaps the first 100 words. Readers who want to continue would need to click through to your site.

BlogBurst

BlogBurst syndicates content from member blogs to the Web sites of metro newspapers like the San Francisco Chronicle, Washington Post, the Austin American-Statesman, and Gannett papers. BlogBurst functions as a wire service, providing the newspaper sites with a rich variety of niche blog content, while giving the blogs wider exposure.

When a reader at the newspaper site clicks on a blog headline, BlogBurst displays the blog post along with advertising. Ad revenue is split with the blogger and the newspaper.

BlogBurst participants must publish their entire blog posts in their RSS feed, not just summaries. The content must be family-friendly, and updated at least once a week.

To enroll, see:

www.BlogBurst.com/blogger/add-blog.html

Protecting your content

The Internet is a great publicity vehicle because it makes your content freely available. By the same token, the openness of the Web makes it easy for people to steal your work. An unscrupulous blogger or Webmaster can copy and paste your most valuable material onto his site within minutes without asking permission.

Every month or so, you should search the Web for some of the text from several of your pages. A Google search for a string of six to eight words within quotation marks should turn up any sites that have copied your content.

A stern message to the owner of the site—or, failing that, the company that hosts the site—usually results in deletion of the stolen material. Here's an example of a cease-and-desist notice you can send via e-mail:

Dear John Doe,

It's come to my attention that you are re-publishing my original content from MySite.com on your Web site, Your-

Site.com. For example, page [ADDRESS] on your site includes the following paragraphs: [TEXT].

Your unauthorized use of my original material violates U.S. and international copyright laws. If the offending material remains available on your site 72 hours from now, I will have no choice but to pursue legal action against you.

Please comply with my request, so that we can remedy this situation without unnecessary difficulty.

Sincerely,

Jane Doe
MySite.com

If no contact information appears on the offending Web site, enter the site's domain name in the search box at:

www.Register.com/retail/whois.rcmx

This will return the name and contact information of the person or company who registered the domain or the site's hosting company. Also try sending your message to webmaster@[domain name] and abuse@[domain name].
Another source of contact information for Web sites is:

www.DomainTools.com

Revenue from your site

A steady audience on your Web site provides additional income opportunities through affiliate programs and advertising. If your site becomes extremely popular, the revenue could be substantial.

Some bloggers report that a combination of affiliate and advertising revenue can result in about 1.5 cents of income for each unique daily visitor to your site. At that rate, a site averaging 1,500 unique daily visitors can generate about $8,200 in annual revenue—not bad for something that requires no ongoing work on your part. Depending on your audience and the type of products related to your niche, you might do better or worse.

New sites usually generate negligible revenue, but advertising or affiliate programs can still be worthwhile. Your audience may appreciate niche advertising, and these programs can boost your visibility with search engines. One option is to donate your affiliate and ad revenues to charities admired by your audience, which sometimes can be handled automatically. The public-relations benefit of donating could outweigh the monetary value, and you won't have to account for it as income and pay tax on it.

In any case, advertising shouldn't overly distract visitors from the main purpose of your site—generating awareness of your business.

Here are some of the leading advertising and affiliate programs authors can use on their Web sites:

Amazon Associates program

Amazon's affiliate program is called Amazon Associates. You can display links for your product and related ones on Amazon, and when your visitors click through to Amazon and make a purchase, you're paid a commission. Typically your commission is a few percentage points of the total sale, depending on the type of merchandise.

Amazon Associates is one of the most familiar and successful programs on the Internet, with more than 1 million member sites. After joining you receive an Associates ID code, which you insert into your links to Amazon products.

After your visitors click on your Associates link, you'll receive commissions on most other purchases those customers make during the following 24 hours. For example, if your visitor buys a plasma TV on Amazon during that same 24-hour session, you'll get a commission on that too.

In 2006 Amazon Associates introduced a new contextual program called Omakase, which displays different products based on the content on your site and your visitor's browsing history at Amazon. The advantage for affiliates is that Omakase is dynamic, exposing your audience to different products each time they visit a different page on your site, increasing the odds of a purchase.

The name Omakase is Japanese for "Leave it up to us," a custom in Japanese restaurants in which the chef improvises a meal based on his knowledge of the diner's preferences.

For more information, visit:

www.Amazon.com/Associates

Commission Junction

Opening an account at Commission Junction provides access to hundreds of niche affiliate programs. You'll find affiliate opportunities for nearly any type of product, including dozens of specialized retailers. The site provides the codes you'll need to insert on your Web site, and consolidated reports of your commissions. See:

www.CommissionJunction.com

eBay

If there's a category of merchandise on eBay of interest to your target market, it may be well worth the effort of opening an affiliate account. You can display relevant ads for popular auctions on your site. The ads contain product information, gallery images, bidding prices, and ending times. eBay claims that the click-through rates for these ads are double that of regular banner ads. After joining, you can operate your eBay affiliate account using a network like Commission Junction, mentioned above.

For more information, see:

http://affiliates.ebay.com

Google AdSense, other advertising

Google's AdSense program is perhaps the best-known Web ad network, and it's relatively easy to sign up and incorporate text or banner ads onto your site. For more information, see:

www.Google.com/Adsense

Two alternatives to AdSense are **www.AdBrite.com** and **www.BlogAds.com**.

Pay-per-click advertising

Unlike with most advertising, with pay-per-click you don't pay fees each time your ad is displayed, but only when someone clicks on your ad and is taken to your Web site. PPC has revolutionized online promotion, and has been wonderfully effective for many Internet businesses. The prime advantage of PPC is its ability to deliver your ad to targeted audiences.

Although PPC can bring targeted traffic to your site, it's unlikely you'll convert enough of those visitors into immediate buyers unless you have unique, high-priced products or services. Google, for example, will charge you 75 cents or more per click for competitive keywords, and only a small fraction of those clicks will result in sales.

Google AdWords

With AdWords, advertisers write short three-line text ads, then bid on keywords relevant to their ad. The ads appear alongside relevant search results or on content pages. For example, to advertise your tropical fish store, you might bid on several different keywords and phrases— **aquarium**, **exotic fish**, **fishkeeping**, and **pet fish**. Depending on how popular those words and phrases are with other advertisers, you might have to pay a minimum of 10 cents, 30 cents, or several dollars for each click. The higher your bid, the higher your ad shows up on the relevant page.

Learn more about Google's AdWords program at:

www.Google.com/Adwords/Learningcenter

You may, however, profit from PPC advertising if you take a long-term view. Do you know how much your customers are worth? If you get any repeat business at all, your customers are worth more than the profit margin from a single sale. If your average customer buys four items during the lifetime of their relationship with you— and your average net profit on those four items is $14 apiece—your average customer is worth $56.

If each of your customers is worth $56, would you spend a few dollars on advertising to attract more new customers?

The most familiar PPC ads are the ubiquitous Google "Sponsored Links" that appear alongside search results or on content-related websites. But Google is no longer the only game in town. Amazon and eBay are jumping into the PPC game, which could present new opportunities for all kinds of businesses.

Businesses who use PPC ads target their customers by bidding on keywords related to what they're selling. For example, if you're selling scuba-diving equipment, you might bid on the keywords **snorkeling** or **diving**. If you bid sufficiently high, your ad will appear on relevant web sites when someone searches for your keyword. You pay for the ad only when someone clicks on it, and the more popular the keyword, the more you'll pay. An obscure keyword might be available for a nickel per click on some networks, while a highly competitive keyword might cost as much as $50 per click.

Until recently, Google AdWords and Yahoo Search Marketing were practically the only alternatives for PPC, with Google commanding a lion's share of the market. But this year things are changing. Just a few short years ago, PPC was called "search engine advertising" because ads were always displayed alongside search results at Google, Yahoo, or another search engine. Sometimes the only thing differentiating your ad from a natural (or organic) search result was the small label "Sponsored Link."

PPC was viewed as a revolutionary way of advertising because you spent money to attract people who had already expressed an interest in what you were selling. In the past couple of years, Google seems to have perfected PPC with its AdWords program. Not only are ads shown alongside search results, but they also pop up on millions of websites—relevant blogs, commerce sites, forums, etc. Like all good things, Google has earned so much money serving up PPC ads that other big Internet players have decided to make a run at it too.

Clickriver

Since advertisers have driven up the bidding on many popular PPC keywords in the past several years, PPC isn't a particularly effective way to sell individual low-priced items. But two new wrinkles have popped up in PPC just recently that is providing new opportunities. First, ad-Marketplace, which had been selling PPC ads exclusively on eBay, has branched out. The program is now open to all online marketers, not just eBay users, and ads may be directed to a variety of sites, including search engines like Ask.com, LookSmart and other shopping-related websites.

Meanwhile, in 2007 Amazon introduced its own PPC network, Clickriver, a system that displays ads on its product detail pages and can be used to direct traffic to your own Web site or anywhere else. One obvious advantage with Amazon's ad network is that it reaches about 60 million registered online buyers. The plain-text ads appear about halfway down product detail pages under the heading "Customers viewing this page may be interested in these Sponsored Links."

First, the good news: Clickriver is much easier to use than Google AdWords. The interface is clean and it responds fast. If you ask for a keyword, your ads begin appearing within seconds. It's also relatively cheap compared to Google because many keywords cost just 10 cents per click. Perhaps the low prices indicate that not many advertisers are competing for the keywords, at least not yet.

Clickriver does a great job of suggesting additional keywords. For example, let's imagine you sell orchid growing supplies. Once Clickriver knows you're targeting orchids, it will suggest every book title and author name in the orchid space, at least those with good sales records. This helps you get your ad in front of the right people. It sounds obvious, but you'd be surprised how many good keywords Clickriver will suggest that you didn't think of.

Keywords aren't the only prospecting tool on Clickriver. You can also target entire categories in Amazon's bookstore in one fell swoop. For example, if you wanted your ad to appear on all Amazon book pages related to "gardening," you'd create a new ad and use the keywords "category gardening."

And now, the bad news: Clicks are very, very sparse with Clickriver. It's very likely that the low click-through rate is because Clickriver ads just aren't that visible on Amazon's detail pages. Visibility will probably always be a tension for this program: For Amazon to make serious money with this, they're going to have to raise the profile of the ads. But the more the ads dominate the page, the more buyers will be distracted from buying the Amazon product they were shopping for in the first place.

The future of PPC

Like many other Internet tools, PPC is evolving at a breakneck pace. So far in this section, we've examined only "keyword-based" PPC systems. But there's a whole other world of PPC that can work for online marketers, and these are known as "product PPC" or "price comparison PPC." Some well-known examples of these are Shopzilla.com, NexTag.com, BizRate.com, Shopping.com, and PriceGrabber.com. It works like this: Participating advertisers upload a list of their inventory. When visitors search for a product, the links to various advertisers show up. Advertisers who pay more are given prominence, but users can also sort the listings to find the lowest price. Each time a visitor buys, the advertiser pays a fee.

It's likely that the competition for PPC advertisers will heat up significantly in the future. Microsoft is also getting into the act, beta-testing a PPC network called MSN adCenter.

Power tools

Part of creating a useful, valuable Web site is understanding the behavior of your visitors—how they find your site, and what they do once they arrive. Depending on which Web host you've selected, you'll have access to some type of traffic reports that can provide valuable insight into which of your content pages are most effective.

If you're doing any paid advertising, these reports can also help you figure out whether your ads are effective. Google Analytics is a very good free tool that provides detailed statistics about the activity of your visitors, and it's fairly easy to add the service to your site. For more information:

www.Google.com/Analytics

Analyzing your traffic

www.MyBlogLog.com is a handy tool for bloggers who want quick statistics on where their visitors are coming from, and what blog posts they click on most often. **StatCounter.com** and **SiteMeter.com** are other free resources for tracking visitor activity at your site.

Linking strategy

Many bloggers publish a list of links to related blogs on their sidebar, known as a *blogroll*. This can be helpful for your visitors, but it can be overdone. You should strike a balance between giving your visitors easy access to useful, outside information, while not encouraging them to leave your site sooner than they otherwise might.

It's counterproductive to link to marginally related sites from your home page because it dilutes your site's "authority" in Google rankings. A better solution is to link to outside content from within individual blog posts when relevant. Build a separate "resources" page on your site where you can point visitors to outside resources without getting penalized for it on your home page.

Search engine optimization

The beauty of publishing a blog is that it naturally optimizes your content for indexing by search engines. A blog makes you highly visible, without your having to think too much about technique. Even so, it helps to know some basics of search engine optimization (SEO) to enhance your site's ability to draw new visitors.

The leading search engines are Google, Yahoo, and MSN.com. If your site doesn't already appear in search results, request that your site be added. To request indexing by the search engines, go to:

- Google: **http://Google.com/addurl.html**

- MSN:
http://Search.MSN.com/docs/submit.aspx

- Yahoo:
  http://Search.Yahoo.com/info/submit.html

Another way to get your site included in the search engines is to have at least one incoming link from another site that's already been indexed by search engines. The next time Google and other search engines crawl the other site, they'll follow the link to yours.

The essential ingredients for a high-ranking site change periodically. Many bloggers and Webmasters waste time and money chasing the "perfect" formula for getting to the top of search results, and then must start over when Google changes the way it evaluates Web pages. Rather than spending lots of time trying to game the system, you can better spend your time adding valuable content to your site.

Keyword density

One effective way to make your content more visible with search engines is *keyword density*. Let's imagine you're writing a blog post about how to wax a car in 30 minutes. You might write the title: "Waxing your car in less than 30 minutes: Here's how." This way, the most important words, *waxing* and *car*, appear at the beginning of the title. Your first sentence might be, "Waxing your car can be a time-consuming chore, but here's how to get it done fast." This reinforces your keywords. Repeating them again will enhance your keyword density and ensure your post ranks high in searches for those keywords.

Be consistent with word choices to maintain keyword density. Let's imagine you have a page on your site devoted to antique Ford Thunderbird cars. Naturally, you'll want *Thunderbird* to appear several times on the page to rank high in search results for that keyword. So you'll want to keep using the word *Thunderbird* instead of slang or nicknames. The sentence "The 1969 *'Bird* was a stylish car" would dilute your keyword density.

Although keyword density makes it easier for your target audience to find you, don't overdo it. If you artificially jam the same keyword several times in each sentence, search engines will detect this and penalize you for "keyword stuffing."

Another way to get penalized with search engines is by participating in so-called "link farms." These are sites that trade or sell Web links, but it seldom works. The only links that will truly boost your site are from high-ranking sites with content similar to yours. So forget about buying links to boost your SEO. Simply produce good content for your audience, and the links and traffic will come naturally.

You've probably seen advertisements for consultants who promise to make your site No. 1 in the search engines within 30 days. Don't waste your money. Chances are, anyone who makes such promises is incompetent, a charlatan, or both.

Your most important links will be from sites in your niche. Links from crowded social sites like MySpace or discussion boards won't strengthen your site's rankings much, says Dave Taylor, author of *Growing Your Business with Google.* "Theoretically all links are good, but I don't believe that links from jungles like MySpace are going to give you any real boost," Taylor says. "Those sites that are easy to get links from just aren't going to have the value of, say, a link from the home page of Stanford.edu or Wiley.com."

Google provides an excellent tutorial for optimizing your Web site:

www.Google.com/Support/Webmasters

The length of your lease

Many factors influencing how much juice your Web site has are outside your immediate control. For example, if your domain is new—registered within the previous year—it will get short shrift in search results. Some experts call this the *Google sandbox effect*, meaning that new Web sites are given a probationary period.

Why would Google penalize new blogs and Web sites? Isn't a new blogger or Webmaster just as capable of producing valuable content? The answer is, newcomers are penalized to help the search engines deal with spam Web sites, a growing problem. Fly-by-night companies build spam sites using stolen content or machine-generated lists of keywords. The spammers sprinkle their sites with Google advertising and make a bit of money, at least until Google wises up and cuts off its ads. To limit their costs, the spammers register their domain for the minimum, one year—they don't want to pay in advance for a site they'll be abandoning soon. Google limits the traffic it sends to new sites to avoid helping these spammers make even more money.

How can you turn this to your advantage? By letting Google and the other search engines know your site isn't spam. Extend your domain registration several years into the future, instead of paying the one-year minimum. By paying your domain registration fees nine years in advance, you'll spend about $90 instead of the minimum $9 for one year. But the $90 investment can provide a big return. Bloggers and Webmasters report huge increases in search-engine traffic just weeks after extending their domain registration for multiple years, according to anecdotal reports.

Privacy policies

If you collect data from your Web site visitors, consider posting a disclaimer. Privacy policies explain how names, addresses, and other information is used or shared with third parties.

The Better Business Bureau provides this suggested outline for privacy policies:

www.bbbonline.org/privacy/sample_privacy.asp

Ethics of online marketing

Perhaps nothing is more important to a business than its reputation. While it's perfectly fine to promote your business energetically, consider the way your promotion might appear to others. Sometimes there's a fine line between being aggressive and being overzealous.

In some cases, the boundaries are clear. For example, the CAN-SPAM Act outlawed unsolicited commercial e-mail, so it's inappropriate to market your company by sending e-mails to strangers. In other cases, you'll need to use your judgment. For example, don't ask people who aren't familiar with your product to review it. And don't review your product yourself.

On the Internet, it's fairly easy to hide your identity, but often it comes back to haunt people who use it as a marketing technique.

Being authentic

Resist the temptation to plant flattering or self-promotion content on the Internet. This sort of behavior is easily detected and the negative reaction can be quick and overwhelming. Being phony on the Internet can quickly cost your company its credibility and the years of work you've spent building a reputation can be damaged.

Damage control

One thing that gives marketers pause about social networking is the lack of control over the conversation. With old media, if a few customers disagreed with a promotional message, a company might receive telephone calls or letters from a few highly motivated individuals. On social networking sites, however, unruly bystanders can create embarrassing situations.

Dell Computer, for example, must endure hostile messages in its MySpace forum from dissatisfied customers. Although these irate postings represent only a tiny fraction of Dell's total customers, those disgruntled customers unhappy with a purchase or service call become highly motivated complainers.

You should promptly acknowledge any critical comments about your product or services as soon as you discover them on any social networking site. Without being defensive, respond directly and honestly, admitting mistakes if appropriate, and the steps you're taking to improve.

Shill reviews

For years it was rumored that several authors and publicists had posted flattering reviews of their own books on Amazon, anonymously. This dishonest tactic of writing shill reviews, sometimes called "astro-turfing," depends on contrived reviews to simulate a grassroots movement for a product on Amazon.

Then in 2004, a computer glitch revealed it was true— the real names of the authors were displayed, earning them a lifetime of embarrassment. One was John Rechy, author of the bestselling novel *City of Night*. The ironic thing was that Rechy was a successful writer whose honors included a PEN-USA West lifetime achievement award. He wasn't famous, but he didn't need shill reviews either. But that computer glitch made him much better known, though probably not in the way he'd hoped.

One medical doctor who has a book for sale on Amazon has submitted hundreds of reviews of other books, which serve primarily to point attention to his own book. Apparently the doctor isn't concerned that his reputation as an author has been tarnished, as he's continued the activity.

In response to years of controversy about abuse of its review system, in 2006 Amazon began requiring that reviewers have an account with a registered credit card before reviews can be submitted. The safeguard prevents individuals from using multiple accounts to submit phony reviews. However, customers aren't required to purchase a product from Amazon before reviewing it.

Spam

This book is intended to encourage ethical and energetic marketing. However, on the Internet, remember that tactics that may seem perfectly fine to you could offend someone else. For example, in 2005 an author sent a series of e-mails announcing his book to a list of addresses harvested from Amazon's Web site. Several recipients were angry enough to post critical reviews of the book and lambaste the author for "spamming." The headline of the book's top Spotlight Review declares, "this author is a spammer." It's not something that will favorably impress potential readers.

142 | Steve Weber

Many consultants encourage entrepreneurs to enter articles about themselves and their products on Wikipedia.org, the popular online encyclopedia. However, the site's guidelines clearly state that Wikipedia is not to be used for personal promotion or to popularize products or Web sites. Articles that are deemed self-promotional are deleted. Likewise, many businesses are promoted on Craigslist.com, an online classified service operated by eBay, in apparent violation of the site's terms of service.

As MySpace has soared in popularity, it has become a magnet for spammers. To deal with a deluge of spam messages, in 2007 MySpace sued Globe.com, accusing that company of sending 400,000 unsolicited, misleading messages to MySpace members. A court ruled Globe.com was liable for $5.5 million in damages—$50 in damages for each message. The company had set up nearly 100 fake MySpace accounts to send random bulk messages to other users. The companies reached a settlement and TheGloble.com agreed to quit using MySpace for "any commercial purpose."

Promote your business relentlessly. But don't do something in the heat of the moment that could damage your credibility. The biggest asset you have is your credibility with the public.

Recommended reading

The New Rules of Marketing and PR: How to Use News Releases, Blogs, Podcasting, Viral Marketing and Online Media to Reach Buyers Directly. By David Meerman Scott, 2007.

Word of Mouth Marketing: How Smart Companies Get People Talking by Andy Sernovitz, 2006.

Citizen Marketers: When People Are the Message by Ben McConnell, 2006.

Duct Tape Marketing: The World's Most Practical Small Business Marketing Guide by John Jantsch , 2007

What No One Ever Tells You About Blogging and Podcasting: Real-Life Advice from 101 People Who Successfully Leverage the Power of the Blogosphere by Ted Demopoulos , 2006.

Blogging for Business: Everything You Need to Know and Why You Should Care by Shel Holtz , 2006.

Buzz Marketing with Blogs For Dummies by Susannah Gardner, 2005.

Naked Conversations: How Blogs are Changing the Way Businesses Talk with Customers by Robert Scoble and Shel Israel, 2006.

Wikinomics: How Mass Collaboration Changes Everything by Don Tapscott , 2006

The Dip: A Little Book That Teaches You When to Quit (and When to Stick) by Seth Godin, 2007

Everything Is Miscellaneous: The Power of the New Digital Disorder by David Weinberger, 2007

The New Influencers: A Marketer's Guide to the New Social Media by Paul Gillin, 2007.

Index

Printed in the United States
144430LV00002B/53/A